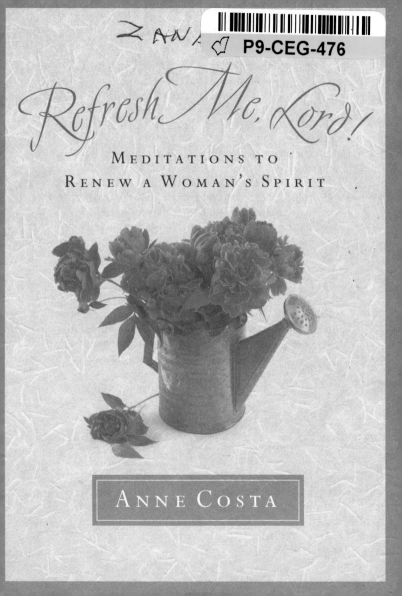

ZANA

P9-CEG-476

Refresh Me, Lord!

MEDITATIONS TO
RENEW A WOMAN'S SPIRIT

ANNE COSTA

The Word Among Us Press, 9639 Doctor Perry Road
Ijamsville, Maryland 21754
www.wordamongus.org
13 12 11 10 09   2 3 4 5 6
ISBN: 978-1-59325-134-5

Unless otherwise noted, Scripture passages contained herein are
from the New Revised Standard Version Bible: Catholic Edition,
copyright © 1989, 1993, Division of Christian Education of the
National Council of the Churches of Christ in the United States.
All rights reserved. Used with permission.
Excerpts from the English translation of the *Catechism of
the Catholic Church* for use in the United States of America,
copyright © 1994, United States Catholic Conference, Inc. –
Libreria Editrice Vaticana. Used with permission.
Cover design by DesignWorks Group

Library of Congress Cataloging-in-Publication Data
Costa, Anne.
 Refresh me, Lord! : meditations to renew a woman's spirit / Anne Costa.
   p. cm.
 Includes bibliographical references.
 ISBN 978-1-59325-134-5 (alk. paper)
 1. Catholic women--Religious life. 2. Christian life--Meditations.
I. Title.
 BX2353.C67 2008
 242'.6431--dc22
                           2008015780

In loving memory of
Anthony A. Cardozo
September 29, 1931 ~ April 7, 2008

"Love you, Daddy <wink>!"

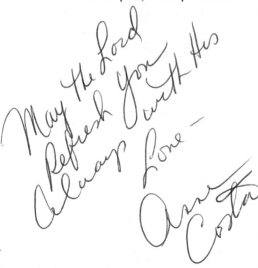

May the Lord
Refresh you with His
Always Love —

Anne
Costa

ACKNOWLEDGMENTS

What a joy it is to be able to publicly acknowledge those people who have been so instrumental in my journey as a Catholic woman and writer. First, I'd like to thank my parents, who have always been there as teachers and who were so committed to passing along the beautiful gift of my faith. For that, I will be forever grateful.

I'd like to thank those who have encouraged and nurtured me along the path of self-acceptance, which has made it possible for me to realize the dream of writing a book, namely: Paul Goggi, who has been my guide, mentor and mirror; my beloved friend and soul sister Susan Heffernan; my spiritual advisor, Father Darr Schoenhofen; and Marti C., Debra C., and Jim P., who have all encouraged me in their own unique way.

I'd like to thank Sue Lindsley for typing the original waterlogged edition of this manuscript, and Donna Davis, the village scribe, for her careful attention to the first edit and her generous words of advice and encouragement.

I am indebted to the many people who shared their hearts and stories with me. They will find themselves in these pages and know who they are. However, I changed names and some details to protect their privacy.

Finally, I'd like to thank my dear sweet husband and hero, Michael, who has always given me the space and support to spread my wings—balanced by his quiet example of the genius of keeping one's feet firmly planted on the ground.

I couldn't conclude without offering a special "shout out" to my precious daughter, Mary Grace, who is God's little spark of heaven in my midst. She has shown patience beyond her years in sharing me with the computer over the course of her life and has been a constant source of inspiration and joy!

And let me finally thank my soul friend and spiritual sister Krista Arduini, who never wavered in her belief that I would be a writer. May she not only have the last word . . . but the last laugh, as well. (Rest in peace, you funny valentine!)

CONTENTS

INTRODUCTION

Refresh me with the light of your presence,
and show me your face as my friend.

—THOMAS À KEMPIS

In his apostolic letter to women, the late Pope John Paul II wrote,

> The moral and spiritual strength of woman is joined to her awareness that *God entrusts the human being to her in a special way.* . . . Thus the "perfect woman" (cf. Proverbs 31:10) becomes an irreplaceable support and source of spiritual strength for other people, who perceive the great energies of her spirit. These "perfect women" are owed much by their families, and sometimes by whole nations.[1]

The exciting truth is that each and every one of us can be a perfectly authentic woman with the potential to bring Christ to others in a unique and defining way.

But we can't do it on our own power. Before we can be a source of spiritual strength for others, we need to take some time for ourselves and allow the Lord to refresh and renew us.

Our lives are busy, our hearts are full, and our minds are often preoccupied with the details and daily responsibilities that surround us; but in the midst of all our activity is the call to embrace a renewed strength in our collective vocation. For no matter what our station in life, our feminine genius is needed.

Refresh Me, Lord! is my gift to you. What began as a dream to write this book almost twelve years ago has grown into a personal mission to encourage, affirm, and inspire women from all walks of life. We are all on this journey together, as we strive to meet the demands of modern living while growing in this most sublime and mysterious vocation of authentic womanhood.

Use this book as a companion on that journey to plug in to the outpouring of God's grace and receive an infusion of his joy. You can read these hundred reflections from cover to cover or simply open the book and read whatever page is right in front of you. The spiritual suggestions at the end of each reflection, labeled "Just for Today," are meant to be a starting point for your personal reflection. You could use them to begin your daily journal entry or share them with others in your conversations. If you are a member of a women's group, the suggestion could be used as an opening topic. If something in the book strikes you as helpful or inspiring, chances are that it will also be of interest to someone else; so pass on what you discover, because we all need spiritual refreshment to keep us going.

It is truly an amazing grace that God is intimately interested in every aspect of our lives. Your heart, your soul, and your spirit are his precious creations, so when you find yourself wanting or weary, remember that the Lord is just a prayer away. He is your friend, always ready, willing, and able to refresh you with the light of his loving presence.

Anne Costa

A Complete Yes

"Here am I, the servant of the Lord;
let it be with me according to your word."

—Luke 1:38

At the beginning of each new year, we often experience stirrings within us that lead us to reflect on where we have been and where we are going. For some, the new year brings feelings of anticipation and excitement; for others, a sense of foreboding or trepidation. Whether facing the beginning of a new year or a new day, each one of us has the opportunity to begin anew and embrace unforeseen experiences. Whatever our plans may be, the mystery of the future remains just that—a mystery.

It is fitting, then, that as Catholics, we set aside days and months throughout the year to reflect upon and celebrate Mary. More than any other person in history, she embraced the mystery of the unknown when she said yes to God at the annunciation. Mary could not have completely understood what was happening to her or how her life would change as a result of the angel's visit. But by her fiat, Mary confirmed her commitment to God and allowed herself to be used by God to redeem humankind. As a result, her entire life became a reflection of the depth of God's love. She expressed awe and wonder at the role she was to play in God's plan of salvation when she proclaimed in the Magnificat, "For he has looked with favor on the lowliness of his servant. Surely, from now on all generations will call me blessed" (Luke 1:48).

Like Mary, each of us has an important part to play in God's perfect plan. We are pilgrim people with a mission to serve in love. May we embrace the unique call God has on our lives with the same receptivity and openness that Mary displayed. We don't have to wait until the beginning of a new year to offer our own complete yes to God. Like Mary, let us walk with God in trust as the mystery of our life unfolds before us.

Dear Lord, lead me along your path of goodness and love. Help me to surrender my plans and projects, just as Mary did, and to say yes to all that you ask of me. ⟶

Just for Today: I will say yes to God.

Bring Him Too

"Go therefore and make disciples of all nations."
—MATTHEW 28:19

A sign on the door of a local church reads, "You are about to participate in the greatest act of worship the world has ever known—the holy sacrifice of the Mass. Be reverent, prayerful, and open to God's grace." Before Mass, the church is usually quiet inside as most people kneel and pray silently. It's a time for collecting ourselves and preparing our hearts for the awesome experience to come. The sign on the door sets the stage and sends a message: something special is about to begin.

As Catholics, we are blessed to be able to participate in the celebration of the Eucharist. Receiving Christ's actual body and blood is a privilege that surpasses any experience on earth. It's so wonderful, in fact, that we shouldn't keep it to ourselves. When we return to our homes and our families, our jobs and our activities, we can share the miracle we have just experienced—we can bring Christ with us into the world.

The time we spend at Mass ought to change us for the better. If others were watching, would they notice a difference in our demeanor, attitude, and actions as we walk out of church? We may not be like Moses, who left the tabernacle of God shining so brightly that he needed to cover himself; we should, however, carry within us a burning desire to share Christ with others.

God has issued an open invitation to each of us to enter into his grace at Mass. As we accept it, we can ask ourselves, How will my encounter with Jesus make me different? How is God's transforming love truly present within me? What does God want to say to the world through me? We already know that the world desperately needs what and whom we experience when we go to Mass. It's up to us to bring Christ to the world, and when we do, the effect will be nothing short of miraculous!

Lord, fill me with your presence each time I attend Mass, so that I might bring you with me to others. ⸺

Just for Today: I will invite Jesus to change me in some way through my participation in the Mass.

Let Go of the Chaos

She looks well to the ways of her household,
and does not eat the bread of idleness.

—PROVERBS 31:27

The enemy of our souls uses many strategies to distract us from accomplishing all that God has planned for us. His tricks of the trade are intended to keep us bound to ill-fated attempts and good intentions. Satan always seeks to strengthen his strongholds, even as Christ pours out his grace to help us overcome them.

One effective tactic is to keep us "drowning in our surroundings." If we are unable to get things done because we are constantly searching for what we need to get started, or if we are mismanaging our time by "flying by the seat of our pants" through life, then we won't reach our maximum potential for God. We can't give our best to the kingdom if we can't clean up the mess in our own homes or make it out the door on time. When we turn to the Lord to help restore the balance and order we need to serve him, we could find ourselves facing some uncomfortable truths buried underneath the chaos in our lives.

Hoarding and disorganization can serve as barriers to intimacy with others and can interfere with our ability to serve the Lord. If we have difficulty letting go of "things," we may find that we are clinging to more than just material goods. Feeling as though we are losing control or becoming overly stressed or even depressed at the thought of cleaning out the closet or putting our affairs in order could mean that our belongings have become tools of bondage. The enemy can then use our possessions and even our emotions to keep us locked in a self-defeating pattern of procrastination and avoidance of the abundant life Christ wants to give us.

Restoring sanity to our life space can become an exercise in spiritual maturity. Reflect on your own patterns, and ask the Lord to guide you in incremental steps toward a more peaceful and contented way of life. Believe that you can have this life, claim it, and—together with Christ—let go of the chaos and clutter, one "thing" and one day at a time.

Lord, thank you for helping me to gain greater self-control and order in my life. Set me free from the bondage of chaos. ⌐

Just for Today: I will choose an area of clutter in my life and begin to bring order to it.

Seeds of Service

*He who supplies seed to the sower and bread for food
will supply and multiply your seed for sowing and
increase the harvest of your righteousness.*

—2 CORINTHIANS 9:10

Second Corinthians 9:10 is exciting! This verse tells us that any seed of service we sow will be multiplied by God to bring about an even greater good than we could have accomplished on our own. Whether we plant a small seed of listening, presence, or respect or give a monetary or material gift, God will multiply it. When we sow the seeds of our gifts and talents in order to serve others, God will complete the harvest by his generous hand.

As we give prayerfully with the faith that our gift will release God's abundance into the situation, then we take the focus off ourselves and place it where it belongs—on God. He is faithful to his promises, and he is the provider of all good things. He will not just honor our actions, but he will exceed our expectations when we sow seeds of service in his name.

This verse also reminds us that God is concerned with even the smallest details of our lives. In the world's economy of scale, the seed is very tiny. And yet, something that begins from a seed—bread—is a basic necessity, the very foundation for our nourishment, both physically and spiritually. Bread, though ordinary in its composition, is the form in which God has chosen to give himself to us through the Eucharist. And he has promised to multiply his goodness through us as we receive him.

God uses us, his laborers in the field, to plant seeds and bring in the harvest of lost or wanting souls. This work of saving souls is not for the fainthearted, yet we don't have to go any farther than the fertile ground of our own families to accomplish it. Jesus lamented in Matthew 9:37, "The harvest is plentiful, but the laborers are few." We are blessed to be among the few.

Lord, thank you for your generous actions and your abundant grace. Show me ways I can serve others so that you can multiply the seeds I plant in your name. ⌒

Just for Today: I will ponder the ways in which God's abundance has touched my life and praise him for the harvest.

Eyes to See With

We look not at what can be seen but at what
cannot be seen; for what can be seen is temporary,
but what cannot be seen is eternal.

—2 CORINTHIANS 4:18

We live in a culture that seems obsessed with visual stimulation. Through television and movies, video games and the Internet, MP3 players and even cell phones, our eyes—the "windows to our souls"—are being exposed to every imaginable sight.

Experts have long suggested that children's behavior can be influenced by seeing violence on television. There can be little wonder, then, that our children's view of the world can be shaped—not to mention harmed—by what they see in the media, too. Day after day, they "see" that material goods are the measure of success, that sex outside of marriage is the norm, that violence is acceptable, that the ends justify the means, and that justice involves getting revenge.

It is up to us to offer our children an alternative—to replace what they are exposed to in the media with a Christ-centered view of the world. True, Christ's view is a countercultural way of looking at life. It not only turns societal thinking upside down, but it places the greatest value on the *un*seen. How can we teach our children to value what we cannot see but know by faith? How can we impress upon them the importance of seeking out where true treasure lies? In what ways are we modeling the art of contemplation in our own lives? How do we communicate our own *interior* vision based on our values, morals, and beliefs that are anchored in the word of God? Ask yourself: How am I actively living out my Catholic world view through my daily actions?

Others may not understand what we believe, but if we live in a committed way, they will know that we are acting upon a different set of priorities. For us, forever is for all eternity, but for the world, it is the time between commercial breaks. Let us pray that our lives will reflect that difference.

Heavenly Father, keep my eyes fixed on you and my heart set on things not of this world, but of the next. Give me courage to bring "what cannot be seen" into the world through my actions. ⌒

Just for Today: I will "look inside" and turn away from excessive visual stimuli.

A Vocation for All Times

"Do whatever he tells you."

—JOHN 2:5

St. Teresa Benedicta of the Cross (Edith Stein) was a Jewish philosopher and convert to Catholicism whose spiritual journey led her to become a Carmelite nun. She was ultimately martyred for her faith in the Auschwitz death camp during World War II and was canonized in 1998. Stein wrote extensively about the proper formation and education of women. With a brilliant mind and humble spirit, she explored and expounded upon the true vocation of women in society. Her wisdom is timely for us today.

Stein related her thoughts about the feminine soul and its expression in vocation in a lecture titled "The Ethos of Women's Professions":

> Any vocation that involves service to others can be considered *feminine*. . . . But the feminine make-up can also adapt itself to essentially masculine vocations. . . . Indeed feminine nature in its purity can embrace all things, and the image of God's Mother at the wedding of Cana is a perfect

example of this: how discretely she prevents the embarrassment of others; how she discerns where there is a need; how she intervenes without being observed. Such a woman is pertinent at all times like a good genius.[2]

Secular movements and conflicting cultural expectations that promised to help women gain validation and a broader sphere of influence in the world have, instead, undermined the importance and value of our God-given femininity. Edith Stein gives us a window into the truth of who God calls women to be. Regardless of the occupation we hold or the role we play in our families and communities, there is inherent dignity and genius in the natural expression of the feminine spirit as it was designed by God. Cultivating an awareness of our feminine souls in light of the charism of Catholic womanhood could truly change our world and add rich meaning to our individual lives.

Lord, help me to understand and embrace my true vocation as a woman in the body of Christ. ⟶

Just for Today: I will have a conversation with St. Edith Stein during my prayer or quiet time.

Holy Face

*All of us, with unveiled faces, seeing the glory of the Lord
as though reflected in a mirror, are being transformed into
the same image from one degree of glory to another;
for this comes from the Lord, the Spirit.*

—2 CORINTHIANS 3:18

St. Jerome said that "the face is the mirror of the mind."[3]
If this is true, then many times a day people can read
our thoughts just by looking at our countenance. These
"mind readers" can be our children, our spouse, our co-
workers, and even strangers we pass on the street. So,
how often do you look in the mirror with the purpose
of seeing the story that is being told by your face?

All of us have an active inner dialogue that we think
we are hiding from the rest of the world. Yet the wisdom of St. Jerome reminds us that we can't always
conceal what is going on inside us. Modern-day moti-
vational speakers and psychologists say that "what we
think, we can become," as proof of the importance and
power of our thoughts and our awareness of them.

Think of a time when you were confused by someone's response to you, or when you felt misunderstood.
In these situations, your face was telling the truth, even

if your words were not. Maybe you were trying to communicate in a caring way, but your face was revealing your internal annoyance or boredom. Or perhaps there is a part of you that wants to connect meaningfully with others, while at the same time, you are fearful of getting too close. In this dilemma, your face can become like a mask with a vacant expression telling others to keep a safe distance away.

Most of the time, we want our countenance to communicate love, acceptance, and sincerity. The beautiful Catholic devotion to the holy face of Jesus helps us to do that. Jesus promises to illuminate us with his light, consume us with his love, and render us fruitful in good works. He also promises to imprint his divine features on our souls and fill us with joy.

Lord, you call us to imprint your holy face on all our thoughts and actions, so that others might see you more clearly. Fill me with the grace to follow that call. ⌁

Just for Today: I will reflect upon the holy face of Jesus.

Who Am I?

*"My soul magnifies the Lord, and my spirit rejoices
in God my Savior."*

—LUKE 1:46-47

Women often struggle to answer the question "Who am I beyond what I do for others?" In our culture, we identify ourselves by the roles we play: wife, working or stay-at-home mom, career woman, volunteer, friend, caregiver, and so forth. Yet a woman's soul cries out for a deeper definition of self. Mary's Magnificat, also known as Mary's Canticle, is in many ways reflective of a woman who discovers her essential purpose. It is a profound proclamation of who she is and the integral part she plays in God's plan of salvation. Reading it in its entirety in the Gospel of Luke (1:46-55) will help us to understand that we, like Mary, cannot define ourselves without speaking of the greatness of God and his relationship with us.

Our souls were made to reflect God. Our fulfillment in this life will come only as we seek to know ourselves as God knows us. This kind of knowing takes time and solitude as well as a trusting openness to God's presence in our prayer life. We can write our own "song of self" through our unfolding relationship with God. He will guide us on our quest for deeper self-awareness and acceptance.

As we strive to offer the deepest parts of ourselves in service to others, we need to reach beyond what we do, to how God desires to express himself through us every day. There is no action too insignificant or too mundane to reflect God's love. Indeed, Mary's entire life was a quiet and hidden unfolding of God's perfect plan for all humankind. The life of each one of us fits into that plan in a unique and essential way. No less important to God is each of our life songs, sung to him with a loving heart. For there is no role we can play that is greater than the one God chooses for us as his beloved daughters.

Heavenly Father, help me to know myself as you know me and to see myself as you see me, so that I may reflect your love to others all the days of my life.

Just for Today: I will read and reflect upon the Magnificat. I will consider writing my own personal canticle to God.

Better to Give

[Remember] the words of the Lord Jesus, for he himself
said, "It is more blessed to give than to receive."

—ACTS 20:35

It's an age-old problem: what do we do when we don't
have enough? Whether it's enough money, enough time,
or enough energy, we always seem to feel that something in our lives is lacking. How we solve the problem
depends on what we think about our world and ourselves. Some people simply go shopping, others go to
war, and still others live without and just make do.

I saw a unique solution to the problem of not having enough as I was driving to work one day. Two boys
about eight years old were locked arm in arm on the
side of a city street. They shared a pair of in-line skates—
one wearing the left skate and one wearing the right—
and together they cruised along the sidewalk. It was
quite a clever solution to the problem of having only
one pair of skates between two boys!

That scene of childhood innocence and ingenuity
illustrates the beauty of giving to others. It also brings
to mind the fact that our usual perspective is often one
of "me first." For instance, when it seems as though

we don't even have the bare necessities ourselves, sharing what little we have with someone else is the last thing we think of doing.

Spiritually speaking, however, we know that when we give out of our own need, we get back so much more than we had to begin with. That's a principle we can count on as long as we are giving according to God's will and with a purity of intention. Those who give generously when they don't have enough themselves are often "richer" than their most affluent neighbors.

The next time that you feel impoverished—whether materially, physically, or spiritually—try not to focus on what you don't have but on giving what you do have to someone else in need. Then, in faith, stand ready to receive the goodness God has to give you in return.

Lord, help me to be generous in the midst of my own poverty. —

Just for Today: I will keep my eyes open for someone in need, and give.

Press On

So let us not grow weary in doing what is right, for we will reap at harvest time, if we do not give up.

—GALATIANS 6:9

One of the greatest spiritual "overachievers" of our time was Blessed Mother Teresa of Calcutta. She accomplished so much, that we might think she rarely took a break from tending to the human misery that surrounded her. However, she spent hours every day before the Blessed Sacrament in adoration of Jesus, who was her source of strength and goodness. In fact, she is quoted as saying, "Do not think that love, in order to be genuine, has to be extraordinary. What we need is to love without getting tired."[4]

What a concept—to love without getting tired. We often don't realize how tired we really are until we have reached the meltdown stage. The mountain of responsibilities before us each day—whether at home, at work, or both—and the demands on our time and attention can be overwhelming. The old adage to "love until it hurts" is sometimes taken too seriously. On top of that, when we fall short of our expectations, we carry a burden of unrealistic guilt. This self-defeating pattern can cause us to "burn out" as a parent, wife, friend, or member of the body of Christ.

Perhaps Mother Teresa's example of giving the first hours of the day to Christ is not practical for you, but maybe giving him the first five or ten minutes could be. Offer your tiredness to the Lord, and ask him to renew your strength for whatever lies ahead of you that day. And make a habit throughout the day of sharing with God your joyful moments as well as your challenges. The Lord, who is always with you, will renew you, so that you can keep going on those very busy days.

The rhythms and responsibilities of our lives will often require us to make adjustments in the amount of effort we put forth. We aren't capable of doing everything—which is as important for us to realize as it is for those who depend on us. But with God's grace, we can cheerfully love and give as much as we are able.

Lord, help me to accomplish my tasks today. Inspire me, energize me, and give me the positive attitude I need to show your love to others. ⎯

Just for Today: I will take time throughout the day to let God renew me.

Choosing Love

And live in love, as Christ loved us.

—EPHESIANS 5:2

Love is always a choice, a decision to be made. Sometimes we are called to choose love in the face of great adversity, persecution, confusion, or pain. At other times, we are called to love through the barren stretches, when our hearts are devoid of emotion or affection. Yet in every case, when we make the decision to love "against all odds," we unleash the power of God in a real and transforming way—not just for those we love, but for ourselves, as well.

When we are open and obedient to the working of the Holy Spirit in our lives, God's love pours into us. It fills us and overflows from us to others. As Catholics, we know that each time we receive Christ in the Eucharist, we say yes to God's love and give God permission to use us for his loving purpose.

One of God's greatest gifts to us is our free will. We are free to love or free to walk away from love. It is as simple as that. But the decision to love is not always simple or easy. Saying yes to love means that our hearts are no longer our own. We embark on a journey that is, as yet, unknown to us. We fear that we might be asked by God to give too much or to sacrifice too much of ourselves in the process. But if we say yes and choose love, the love of God will transform us.

A couple who has been married for twenty years was asked if they had a secret for staying happily married. They agreed that the secret was a lesson they had learned in their Pre-Cana classes. Simply put, the lesson was that "love is a decision." They consciously made that decision every day of their lives, even when it wasn't easy. But they've never regretted it for a moment. And as the years have gone by, their love has grown beyond what they ever could have imagined.

The critical choice to love or not to love confronts each of us every day. Christ asks us to risk everything by choosing love. He is waiting for our reply. . . .

Heavenly Father, give me the courage to say yes to love and to be transformed each day by your power. —

Just for Today: I will make a conscious decision to love against the odds.

True Contentment

*"So do not worry about tomorrow, for tomorrow
will bring worries of its own."*

—Matthew 6:34

Each morning, as we contemplate the tasks and demands
that face us, it is good to remember that we are exactly
where God calls us to be at that moment. Our lives are
unfolding "on schedule," and we don't have to worry
about where we "should" be. If we focus too much on
where we've been, where we think we ought to be, or
where we want to be in the future, we miss the opportunity to be used as God's instrument where we are. In fact,
if we take the time to look, there is beauty to be found
in the lessons and rhythms of the moment-to-moment
experiences that are unique to each one of us.

This is the temptation: to worry and second-guess
ourselves and God. We start to wonder whether we
are really on the right track, or whether we are missing
out on some major blessing that seems to be just out of
reach. We grow restless when our expectations seem to
be different from God's will. It is always good to discern our direction, but putting too much energy into
the regrets and rejections of yesterday or the wishes

and worries of tomorrow will keep us from being "present and accounted for" today and cause us to miss out on what God can do in our lives right now.

G. K. Chesterton wrote, "True contentment is a real, even active virtue—not only affirmative but creative. It is the power of getting out of any situation all there is in it."[5] Think of the magnificent potential of the present moment! When we go with the flow and trust that whatever God has planned for us today is exactly as it ought to be, then our spirits will be content, and we will experience a deep fulfillment and freedom. Regardless of what you think your life ought to be like today, remember that God can make the most out of every moment, as you live in the present with him.

Lord, help me rest in your will for me today and experience the true contentment of trusting in you.

Just for Today: I will let go of my thoughts of yesterday and my plans for tomorrow. I will strive to experience this day, moment by moment.

Love Lives

"Give, and it will be given to you. A good measure, pressed down, shaken together, running over, will be put into your lap; for the measure you give will be the measure you get back."

—LUKE 6:38

How important is it for us to give? So important, that Thomas Merton said, "Love can only live by giving."[6] In truth, one way that Christ's love is kept alive in our world today is through our daily acts of giving. Whether we are making tiny hidden sacrifices or larger public ones, we are advancing the kingdom of God and the cause of love.

The culture of materialism and abundance in which we live constantly challenges us to maintain our focus. Over time, what we possess can begin to possess us. The more things we acquire, the more we seem to want or think we need. We are constantly bombarded by images of the newest, biggest, best item that the retail world has to offer. Love can get lost as we begin to define ourselves by the material things that surround us. This climate of greed and insecurity can choke off the life of love, sacrifice, and service that is so vital to the human spirit.

In Luke's gospel, Jesus tells us that the more we give to others, the more we will receive from God. Of course, he wasn't referring just to material things (although people sometimes report that their businesses improve after they give more than they thought they were able to). What we get from God in return for our giving to others is the peace, love, joy, and restoration for which our souls long. God offers us his eternal security, which is far more valuable and enduring than anything we can accumulate or cling to here on earth.

We can give in spite of our tendencies toward selfishness, and we can overcome the temptation to hoard what we have. By God's grace, we can bring love to life in our world today with one generous and unselfish act of giving. So go ahead. Give a little bit, and see what "good measure" your heavenly Father returns to you!

Lord, give me the courage and conviction to let go of the things that are blocking the flow of love in my life, so that I can receive a generous helping from you. ⎯

Just for Today: I will "clean house" and give away something I have been clinging to.

Amazing Grace

For you were called to freedom, brothers and sisters;
only do not use your freedom as an opportunity
for self-indulgence.

—GALATIANS 5:13

Let's face it: most of the time, the lofty ideals of our inner spiritual life have little to do with our day-to-day living. We still holler at our kids, grumble about our jobs, and jostle for first place in the checkout line. I don't know about you, but if I really listened to my inner voice, I'd hear it saying, "If all these people would just leave me alone, then I could really be holy!"

This is the truth of the human condition, the separation between what we wish to do and what we really do. It is also why grace is so amazing. St. Paul lamented about this inner conflict when he wrote, "I do not understand my own actions. For I do not do what I want, but I do the very thing I hate. . . . I can will what is right, but I cannot do it" (Romans 7:15, 18). We all struggle with the same bondage, yet St. Paul said that we should live in the Spirit and remember that we have been called to live in freedom.

Spiritual freedom is the only genuine freedom, and it flows directly from our submission to the Holy Spirit. It is different from the worldly "freedom" that feeds our carnal natures and requires that our every whim be satisfied. God's freedom comes from doing what is right, not just once, but as a lifelong commitment. Each of us is on a journey of spiritual maturity that will lead us to greater freedom in Christ. Our guide on this journey, the Holy Spirit, doesn't force us: he respects our free will but gently leads us step by step toward perfect love.

Perfect love. That is what our hearts truly long for and what we aspire to as followers of Christ. Little by little and day by day, we grow deeper in the Spirit of God, and that is truly amazing grace. So let's not lament, but instead lay down whatever stands in the way of reaching the holiness for which we long.

Lord, thank you for your Spirit of grace that leads me to a deeper life of love and holiness. ⟶

Just for Today: I will accept my shortcomings, confess them, and press on toward perfect love and freedom.

Covenant of Caring

For the LORD *gives wisdom;*
from his mouth come knowledge and understanding.

—PROVERBS 2:6

When you were trying to help someone in need, did you ever find yourself keeping an emotional or physical distance from them in order to protect your own emotional well-being? In his book *Creative Ministry,* Henri Nouwen writes that these masks we hide behind create artificial barriers that can alienate others and make them feel misunderstood.[7] Whether we are tending to the needs of our children, our spouse, our friends, or people outside our inner circle, Nouwen stresses that genuine healing can only take place when two people enter into a sincere heart-to-heart encounter. At this heart level, our connectedness with one another enters into covenant and releases the power of love that can make us whole.

Entering into a covenant of caring with others doesn't depend on how smart or talented we are. In fact, we may give someone what we think is a brilliant piece of advice, only to be met with a blank stare. This is because we are called to be open on a deeper level—to another way of knowing, a different kind of wisdom. It is the wisdom of the Holy Spirit. It can fill us, guide us, and call forth the healing love of Jesus to flow through us to others. The Spirit knows more than we ever could about the needs of others. This type of understanding is what a hurting heart needs most.

When we encounter paralysis of spirit, blindness of heart, or the hemorrhaging of humanity in others, it is good to reflect on how Jesus responded. He met people where they were with an abiding presence of compassion as he fixed his eyes on the Father. We are called to do the same. The courage of compassion requires that we face our own fears with as much honesty and authenticity as we possibly can. We can shed our masks more easily when we accept and make peace with our own limitations and vulnerabilities. Then we will be free to enter into a covenant of caring that will reflect the love and life of Christ right where we are.

Lord, remove the barriers that keep me from entering into authentic relationships with others. ⟶

Just for Today: In the middle of a difficult decision or situation, I will stop and seek the wisdom of the Holy Spirit first.

Prayer and Action

The prayer of the righteous is powerful and effective.

—JAMES 5:16

It's tempting to underestimate the power of prayer. We tend to think that we only serve others by "doing"—after all, actions are tangible, and most often, so are their effects. But as St. James reminds us, we can also be effective servants through our interior life of prayer:

> Are any among you suffering? They should pray. Are any cheerful? They should sing songs of praise. Are any among you sick? They should call for the elders of the church and have them pray over them, anointing them with oil in the name of the Lord. The prayer of faith will save the sick, and the Lord will raise them up; and anyone who has committed sins will be forgiven. Therefore confess your sins to one another, and pray for one another, so that you may be healed. (James 5:13-16)

Thomas Merton described the interdependence of action and prayer in terms of the intermingling of a spring and a stream. "Unless the waters of the spring are living and flow outward," he wrote, "the spring becomes only a stagnant pool. And if the stream loses contact with the spring which is its source, it dries up."[8]

In Merton's beautiful image, prayer is the spring of living water, and action is the stream that flows out from it to others; for both are borne of the same water. However, if action is out of touch with an interior source of prayer, it eventually becomes arid and barren; and prayer that does not overflow into action is cut off from life. This is the integrity of prayer and action.

Author Emilie Griffin wrote that prayer "is not to be taken on with a mentality of success." "The goal in prayer," she explained, "is to give oneself away."[9] We give ourselves away in prayer by offering our time, our full attention, and a song of praise to God in the silence of our hearts. As we serve God and others through our prayer, the fruit and integrity of our actions will bring great help and healing to others.

Lord, may the living waters of your Spirit enrich my life, so that my prayer and actions are a reflection of your love that flows freely to others. ⟶

Just for Today: I will start and end my day with a time of silent prayer.

One Bold Step

I hereby command you: Be strong and courageous;
do not be frightened or dismayed, for the LORD your God
is with you wherever you go.

—JOSHUA 1:9

The legend of Veronica tells of a woman who stepped
out of the safety and anonymity of the crowd to offer
a small gesture of compassion toward Jesus on his way
to the cross. She took a great risk in confronting the
outrageous spectacle of violence and suffering that was
unfolding before her. She allowed herself to be moved
into action, to wipe the bruised and beaten face of
our Lord, when the "comfortable" thing to do would
have been to remain hidden and numb. Not content to
remain a mere spectator on the sidelines, Veronica is
certainly a model for our times.

In our world today, we are bombarded by images
of suffering. Some are far away, and others may be
right in our own families. We can easily become overwhelmed with the negativity of it all and think that our
quiet daily gestures of compassion couldn't possibly
make a difference. Jesus, even in the throes of his passion, revealed through Veronica that when we make
even one small gesture of charity toward another, we

magical or superstitious, but because there is life in the Holy Spirit and in God's word.

If your child is struggling in a certain area, find a simple Scripture passage that will encourage, such as "The Lord is my helper; I will not be afraid" (Hebrews 13:6). If your teenager is worried about the future, share Jeremiah 29:11: "For surely I know the plans I have for you, says the LORD, plans for your welfare and not for harm, to give you a future with hope." For those times when you don't know what to say, let the Holy Spirit say it through the Scriptures. Many verses, especially in the psalms, are power packed with truth that can help us through a difficult day. Even when the day is going smoothly, speaking God's word in faith holds promise for making it an extraordinary day in the Lord!

Lord, thank you for your word, which counsels and comforts me in times of need. Give me the courage to share it with others. ⸺

Just for Today: I will ask the Holy Spirit to guide me in claiming a Scripture verse to study and take to heart.

A Little Lesson

"How much more will your Father in heaven give good things to those who ask him!"

—MATTHEW 7:11

On a recent visit to my daughter's elementary school, I received a lesson in giving that I won't soon forget. After walking her to her classroom, I prepared to leave the building through the front door. As I approached the exit, I saw a mother with her tiny son coming toward me, so I stepped aside to let them through. The little boy, probably no more than three years old, came bursting through the door, dragging his mother behind him. All of a sudden, he broke away from her grip and sprinted back toward the door, which was just closing behind them.

"Where are you going?" his alarmed mother cried. The boy didn't immediately answer, because he was busy wrestling with the heavy door. He had, in fact, thrown his whole body weight against the door and was just catching his breath, when he proudly proclaimed, "I'm holding the door for the lady!" I looked down at this little figure and saw that he was beaming from ear to ear, full of excitement over his accomplishment.

"What a gentleman! You've just made my day!" I called out, as he scampered off with his very proud mom.

That little boy taught me in a simple way that it is truly the natural desire of our hearts to reach out to others and help them. Our giving flows from the very presence of God within us. He is, above all, a God who is "bursting at the seams" with good things to give! If we go through our lives acting on that impulse to give, we can tap into the wellspring of sheer delight that is the fruit of our action. Spontaneous and heartfelt expressions of caring can greatly improve the quality of our lives, because thinking about somebody else's needs before our own gives meaning, texture, and depth to our existence. That little fellow may never know how his tiny gesture of caring ignited my heart that day. It prompted me to extend the kindness to others and to take delight in each tiny act of giving, just as God does.

Lord, fill me with wonder and delight today and always, as you give to others through me. ⸺

Just for Today: I will surprise someone with a gift.

God's Call

*"I have said these things to you so that my joy may be
in you, and that your joy may be complete."*

—JOHN 15:11

God's call is a call to excellence. It is a call to embrace
beauty in all its splendor and sorrow in all its agony. It
is a call to the deepest depths and the widest breadth of
our fragile and awesome humanness. We are called to
an awakening to the life that is in each present moment,
feasting with our eyes and with our heart stretched
wide open with expectation.

We are not to settle for anything less than the complete offering of God's joy for our journey. St. Teresa
of Ávila said, "You pay God a compliment by asking
great things of him." He lovingly and carefully plants
our deepest desires within us, so that we might seek
to be filled by him. He desires our whole presence and
full attention at this grand affair that is life—this life,
this one life.

Let us not be distracted or detoured by the lesser
things, the imposters and the counterfeit joys that surround us. We can cast aside the quick fixes and cheap
thrills and revel in the kingdom of God that is at hand!

Indeed, we are told by Jesus that it is within us. He is within us, and the banquet he is preparing is nothing less than spectacular. God's call is not a call to self-indulgence and decadent living. It is not a life of consumption and grandiosity, but a life of communion and grace.

God's desire is to give us great things, small as we are. These are the miracles of our lives—that his strength is made full in our weakness; that to gain our lives, we must lose them; that the least among us is the greatest in his sight; and that in the midst of it all, we are loved and chosen and called to be his very own and to share in his complete joy!

Lord, help me to live each day to the fullest, in the fullness of your most excellent love. ⟶

Just for Today: I will allow myself to be wooed by the wonder of each moment and embrace the gift of joy that God desires to give me today.

Just One

*What gain have the workers from their toil? I have seen the
business that God has given to everyone to be busy with.
He has made everything suitable for its time.*

—ECCLESIASTES 3:9-11

Over commitment is really no commitment at all.
Filling our lives to the breaking point with projects
and becoming overextended at work or at home can
leave us spread too thin to fully commit to anything. A
genuine commitment requires patient endurance, fidel-
ity, attention, and a willingness to give our whole self to
another person or situation. In other words, commitment takes a good deal of time and calls us to cultivate
a history of presence with a person or a cause. We
can't rush, preoccupied with what we have to do next,
and expect to make a true commitment to what we're
doing now.

Balance is a gift we can give ourselves in the face
of the demands placed on us for immediate results.
Taking time to discern how we will spend our valuable
time each day and how we will expend our precious
energy is essential for our own well-being and for
the good of those around us. Dr. James Dobson, a

prominent Christian psychologist, believes that one of the leading causes of the breakdown of the family is that people are simply *too tired* to tend to the commitment they have made to one another.[10] There will always be unlimited choices to act on and causes to champion. There will always be one better thing to do, one more good idea to pursue. But we have to stop and ask ourselves, "Should I?"

To help us in our struggle for balance, we can follow the example of Mother Teresa, who said, "I can only love one person at a time. I can only feed one person at a time. Just one, one, one."[11] It is true with us also; we have only one husband, one family, one life. Let's rearrange our focus to the one person or thing that is right in front of us. Let us seek wisdom to pace ourselves and give the gift of time and presence that leads to a lasting and true commitment.

Lord, *"teach us to count our days / that we may gain a wise heart"* (Psalm 90:12). ——

Just for Today: I will examine my priorities and adjust my schedule accordingly.

In the Name of the Lord

For our struggle is not against enemies of blood and flesh,
but against the rulers, against the authorities, against
the cosmic powers of this present darkness, against the
spiritual forces of evil in the heavenly places.

—Ephesians 6:12

Healing begins in the heart. No matter what we are going through physically, God works within our hearts to bring us into a deeper knowledge and closer union with him. All human brokenness stems from our separation from him. So it is hard to understand how we have come so far as to be discouraged from speaking the name of the Lord in the helping professions and healing institutions that have been established to make people well.

Since God created us in his own image as creatures of mind, body, and spirit, we can offer healing in the name of the almighty physician, healer, and counselor. Today, however, the power of science and technology has been elevated over the reality of God's dominion in the realm of healing—not that the two are in opposition, but one is subject to the other. Science and technology are not intrinsically bad, but in the forced absence of God's sovereignty, they run the risk of becoming idols and religions of their own. More and more, we see the moral, ethical, and natural laws of the Judeo-Christian tradition being systematically replaced with new age, secular, humanistic views in the name of "progress" at all costs.

This "progress" has the capacity to do great violence to the human spirit, and it is not pleasing to God. Whether we are in a healing profession or not, we face the challenge and vocation of keeping God at the center of our actions and the Holy Spirit as the guide for our decisions. To help us, we can quietly offer spiritual communions throughout the day to rededicate our actions to the healing power of God in our lives. Let us pray that all of our healing efforts be in the name of Jesus Christ our Lord.

Lord, use me as your healing instrument. Let me speak your name through my actions today and always. ⌐

Just for Today: I will take a quiet moment to rededicate my healing efforts in the name of Jesus.

Life Bearers for Christ

"Blessed is the fruit of your womb."

—LUKE 1:42

Women are called to be life bearers in many different ways. We are created to bring forth life, not just physically, but emotionally, spiritually, and artistically as well. Just like Mary, who bore Life himself, we have the capacity to bring glory to God and to magnify his goodness.

What does it mean to give life spiritually, emotionally, or artistically? It means we embrace our procreative, God-given, feminine attributes and bring them to bear on our interactions with others. For example, we all know that women are rich in their emotions. Our emotional lives are made in the image of the deep emotionality of Christ, who wept, pitied, and was amazed. He was also deeply troubled and angered while he was here on earth. As a human being just like us, he no doubt experienced all the emotions we do.

However, Jesus was never *ruled* by his emotions as we sometimes are. His emotions were subject to the divine will of his Father and were brought to life through his relationship with him. Since women are essentially relational in our nature, we are the ones who are especially equipped to bring forth life through our emotions, spirits, and talents.

Think of a way in which you have nurtured the life of another through the expression of your emotions. Ponder a time when you have given birth to an idea that has helped you or someone else to grow spiritually. Recall a time when you labored to cultivate a budding relationship or to create something new. All of these examples speak to the ways in which we are uniquely called to be life bearers in our vocation as women in the body of Christ.

While it's important for us to remember that giving birth physically is not our *right*—it is the sole prerogative of God and is his precious gift to us—we have the responsibility to take our role as life bearers seriously in whatever way we are called. Our cooperation with God's will for our bodies, minds, emotions, spirits, and special talents will truly reflect and bring the miracle of God's life to others.

Lord, thank you for the vocation of life bearer. Make me worthy of the call. —

Just for Today: I will reflect on how I am called to bring life to others.

God's Child

I have calmed and quieted my soul,
like a weaned child with its mother.

—PSALM 131:2

Some people have vivid memories of early childhood, recalling specific events or experiences with great clarity. I am not one of those people! When I try to remember anything about being a very young child, I draw a blank, with the exception of one very precious and powerful memory.

I was about three years old, and I remember being rocked to sleep in my mother's arms. I'm told it was something that happened quite often, so the memory is probably the recollection of all those intimate moments spent just before falling asleep. Yet, I clearly remember one night in particular.

My mother was quietly singing my favorite song, "Three Little Fishies," as she rocked me. I can still hear the creak of the maple rocker on the hardwood floor of my bedroom; I even remember the way the light from the hallway cast a golden stripe on the wall. But what I remember most of all is the warm feeling I had inside and the tenderness of my mother's touch. It was like being in the safest place in the world.

Psalm 131 compares God's love to the love between a mother and a weaned child. It is a powerful yet tender image of God that most of us can relate to, both as mothers and daughters. A weaned child has been fed and is satisfied. There is no "functionality" between the mother and the child; they are both free to simply enjoy the other. In our relationship with God, we sometimes tend to go to him only when we need something, instead of just enjoying his presence. Also, a satisfied child is not bothered by distractions or dependencies. The attachment to the mother is pure and complete. If this doesn't sound like your relationship with God, ask yourself, In what areas of my life am I still restless or unsatisfied? What do I need to be weaned from in order to be completely at rest with God? How does God desire to comfort me? What stands in his way?

Lord, thank you for your loving embrace. Help me to let go of every distraction and attachment and find rest in you. ⁓

Just for Today: I will reflect on a memory of when I experienced God's comfort and care in a special way.

Holy Laughter

There is nothing better for them than to be happy and enjoy themselves as long as they live.

—ECCLESIASTES 3:12

Have you ever seen the pictures of Christ laughing? One artist in particular draws Jesus throwing his head back in what appears to be a complete belly laugh. Viewing that picture makes me wonder which one of the disciples might have caused that reaction in our Lord!

Somewhere along the way, maybe in the Dark Ages, we got the idea that to be good Christians, we had to be serious and pious all the time. Laughter was reserved for such irreligious endeavors as feasts and festivals, and wasn't a regular occurrence in everyday life. We can be thankful that we don't live in such times anymore and that we can even laugh in church when there are humorous moments. We've come a long way in appreciating the value and beauty of laughter.

A poet might imagine laughter as an echo of God's love. For one mother in the Bible, it became the name of her long-awaited son, Isaac (Isaac means "he will laugh"). For some, laughter has been a proven elixir and has healed bodies, minds, and souls. Truly, laughter is an exercise in spiritual "expansion" that could be considered an act of worship.

Our routines can sometimes "stiffen our souls" and cause us to lose the sense of wonder and delight that is natural to us. Just look at children. They live for the moment, laughing easily and heartily. They can be carried away by the slightest whim and let out an ear-splitting shriek of joy that can be heard on the other side of heaven. Guess what? We used to be like that.

So let's not take ourselves too seriously. Look for lighthearted moments in your day, and share them with others. Give the gift of playfulness to those around you. Laughter surely draws us closer to God's heart. Did you ever think that when God finished creating heaven and earth and Adam and Eve and had proclaimed, "It is very good!" that he just might have let out a big hearty laugh, the echo of which we can still hear in the gift of our own laughter today?

Lord, give me a childlike spirit, and help me to laugh today! ⟶

Just for Today: I will share a lighthearted moment with someone and savor the warmth it brings.

Pruning with a Purpose

*"Every branch that bears fruit he prunes
to make it bear more fruit."*

—John 15:2

Jane raised her four children as a stay-at-home mom, against society's expectations that she also pursue a career outside the home. Her dream had always been to become a wife and mother, and she never aspired to apply her many talents anywhere other than in her home, for the benefit of her family. So when Jane was faced with an empty nest, she was at a loss. What began as a nagging feeling of emptiness turned into a crippling sense of insecurity and fear of the future.

Jane felt completely incapable of making the changes that she knew she needed to make in order to experience the next season of her life. She had lost her identity and her purpose, and she felt the sting of inadequacy deeply. A battle brewed within her against bitterness, as she struggled to find a new direction and focus for her life.

That struggle led Jane to seek spiritual direction from a priest. She was surprised when he told her that she was about to enter the most fruitful time of her life. He explained that God often allows us to experience a deep loss or loneliness to make us ready to receive what he wants to give us next. Jane was going through a physical and spiritual pruning that would lead to a different type of success in her life.

Since Jane had mostly involved herself with tasks and roles that made her feel competent and complete, she did not often feel the need to rely on Christ as the center of her life. Pruning became necessary to enable her to experience Christ in a deeper way. Now her "work" would be of a spiritual nature, as she learned to lean on Jesus and trust in him for the next steps on her journey.

We will all experience the pruning power of God. It's important for our growth and fruitfulness. Then we will learn the same loving lesson Jane did. What she thought was a tragic and sad ending became the brand-new beginning of a more active and gratifying communion with Christ in her life.

Lord, may the pruning in my heart lead me to a deeper communion with you. ⟶

Just for Today: I will reflect on how the Lord's pruning has helped me to grow.

Holding On

Then he said to them, "I am deeply grieved, even to death; remain here, and stay awake with me."

—MATTHEW 26:38

A woman recounted her experience of undergoing the rigors of chemotherapy to defeat breast cancer. Halfway through the grueling regime, she hit a wall of despair. Knowing what she had just gone through and facing what was yet to come was almost too much to bear. As she waited for the oncologist, the woman turned to her daughter, who had been at her side from the very beginning, and confided through a torrent of tears, "I'm afraid. I don't know if I should stay and face this or just walk away."

Hearing her mother's agonizing indecision, the daughter, without hesitation, embraced her as they cried together. She didn't rush her mother or press for a decision but just held on tight. The daughter waited patiently for her mother's lead. Then, drawing strength from the well of her daughter's compassionate heart, the mother said, "I'm going in!" They walked in together, arm in arm, ready to face the next round of chemo.

More than anything else, people need this kind of solidarity in their suffering. They need to know that no matter how hard it gets or how ugly it becomes, we are going to hold on to them and not let go. They need the reassurance that we will not be frightened away by their vulnerability and confusion, and that no matter what, we won't disconnect in order to spare ourselves the pain of watching them suffer.

This kind of staying power requires courage that can only come from the Lord. We can't do it on our own. With Mary at the foot of her son's cross as our model, we can ask ourselves these questions: How can we commit ourselves to be a source of strength in the lives of people who are suffering? How can we communicate our willingness to hold on for dear life and go where they go, so that they will never have to go there alone? What must we do to overcome our fear?

Lord, give me the grace and the courage to face suffering and stay connected to those who suffer. —

Just for Today: I will hold on when I'd rather let go.

Reaching Out

*"Just as you did it to one of the least of these who are
members of my family, you did it to me."*

—MATTHEW 25:40

Many of the townsfolk were amused by her childlikeness; others mocked and taunted her. She rode through town on a rickety old bicycle, talking wildly to herself as she went about her daily routine of collecting cans and cigarette butts. Nearly every day, she would sit on a bench in the center of town, blowing bubbles for hours. That's why everyone called her "The Bubble Lady."

She was grist for the gossip mill and strangely accepted as a town mascot. When I tried to find someone who could tell me her name or something about her, no one could. I decided to make it my mission to learn more about her. What I learned was no laughing matter.

Lola (not her real name) had spent most of her life on the streets. She was indeed a simple soul, who was mentally impaired and probably also an alcoholic. The bruises and scars on her body told the story of a life of dangerous entanglements on the fringes of society. Still, she had the heart of a child. She lived in a closet-size room crammed full of belongings collected from the curb. The grimy walls were lined with sketches in pencil and crayon that she had drawn by hand. Their skillfulness belied her childlike demeanor. Her most cherished possession was a sketch she had drawn of her childhood home. It was the only thing she had left of the "good old days."

Simple as she was, Lola taught me a lot. She taught me about the strength of vulnerability and the terrible effect that devaluation has on the lives of people who are poor and discarded. She challenged my hidden assumption that people "bring it all on themselves," and she showed me what it is like to live in a world where no one knows your name. I learned to never *ever* judge others, because we simply have no idea what their lives are really like. Above all, she taught me how to reach out to someone who is different from me. When I did, I found someone who was truly worth knowing and loving. Thanks, Lola.

Lord, watch over your most vulnerable ones, and give us the courage to reach out to them in love. —

Just for Today: I will reach out.

A Special Meeting

*"O Lord, you have searched me and known me. . . .
and are acquainted with all my ways."*

—Psalm 139:1, 3

More than anything else, women want to be understood.
We want to be known, not superficially, but on the deepest levels, through a meaningful and intimate embrace
and acceptance of our hearts. These longings are essentially feminine, borne out of our sensitive natures and
our intuitive impulses to seek what is whole and not dis-
sect something into its parts. Women are infinitely and
miraculously more than the sum of our parts, and we
desire to be known and understood in this way.

These longings, when purified, nourish and nurture
life. They lead us to be concerned with the dignity of
the whole person, to look beyond what is seen to the
unseen essence of others. However, when these longings are not purified, they get distorted and can lead
us into disappointment and pain. Such was the case
with the woman at the well.

Described only as "the Samaritan woman," she had
a long history of broken relationships in her quest for
authentic intimacy. Her actions brought both shame

and isolation to her life. Even her midday encounter with Jesus would have been considered scandalous, because at that time women did not speak to men in public. Moreover, their ethnic backgrounds would have prohibited any kind of contact. Essentially, the two never should have met.

How amazed the woman must have been when Jesus began to talk with her. How much more surprised she must have been to discover that standing before her was a man who knew everything about her. He could read her heart and touch her very soul. Deeper than any romance she had experienced, this encounter touched her hidden longings and revealed how they could be fulfilled. Jesus understood her to the core.

Like the Samaritan woman, we are invited to drink deeply from the well that is Jesus. He knows us, understands us, accepts us, and loves us. He wants to have a special meeting with us every day. Listen as he speaks to you today.

Lord, you know me better than I know myself. Thank you for speaking to my heart and understanding my every need. ⸺

Just for Today: I will seek an intimate dialogue with Jesus.

Slow and Steady

There are those who work and struggle and hurry,
but are so much the more in want.

—Sirach 11:11

For as long as I can remember, I have gone through life as if I were perpetually late for an urgent appointment. Always on the move, I can never get there fast enough. Everything I do is at an accelerated pace; I eat fast, walk fast, and if I could, I'd probably find a way to sleep fast! Consequently, I've spent most of my life racing toward some imaginary finish line. On most days, I feel as if I'm going in circles!

This condition has caused me trouble in the past, but I've learned to lighten up and accept it with humor. For instance, there's a homemade sign in my office that reads, "Slow and steady wins the race!" I can even say that I appreciate the logic of including the turtle in the animal kingdom, and lately I have deliberately taken the long way home just to prove that nothing earth shattering will happen if I follow this leisurely route.

Charles E. Hummel warns that "the danger in life is permitting the urgent thing to crowd out the important."[12] With the help of the Holy Spirit, I am learning that just because I feel an internal sense of urgency, doesn't necessarily mean I have to act on it. Taking the time for reflection reminds me to seek God's will first, instead of reacting with my own. It's a lesson I can hardly afford to rush.

The Lord has given me an image to help me. In it, he is sitting at the wheel of a pace car in front of the roaring engine of my will. Most of the time, the yellow flag of caution is waving to slow me down to a safe pace. Only after a few laps of prayer does the green flag wave me on to "full speed ahead." I'm learning, but I have a long way to go. With God's grace, I will remember to take the scenic route and enjoy the ride!

Lord, help me to pursue what is important to you over what is urgent to me, and grant me the wisdom to know the difference. ⸺

Just for Today: I will take the long way.

A Good Fight

I have fought the good fight, I have finished the race,
I have kept the faith.

—2 TIMOTHY 4:7

Don't let anybody tell you that the path of Christianity is for the weak or faint of heart. St. Paul's words to Timothy remind us that there will be times when our faith will be tested, and we will be called on to put up a good fight. We will have to battle temptations, fatigue, distractions, sin, and a host of other things throughout our lives. Some days we will feel like throwing in the towel or holding up the white flag in surrender. "Enough!" will be our inner plea; "Lord, just take me now!"

Any long-distance runner will tell you about the "wall"—that moment in the race when the runner's mind and body scream in unison to just give up. Yet if the runner pushes on, even just a few steps more, she will catch her second wind. It is as if her feet take flight, and she breaks free from the chains of exhaustion to be renewed in strength and spirit. This same principle applies to our walk of faith. Just when we think we have reached the breaking point, we can push through to a higher level of spiritual growth or closeness with Christ.

This breakthrough comes when we resolve to stay in the race for the long haul. At the end, St. Paul reminds us, there is a crown of righteousness reserved for each one of us. He also says that no matter what battle we are waging on earth, "the Lord will rescue [us] from every evil attack and save [us] for his heavenly kingdom" (2 Timothy 4:18).

Keep in mind that we never have to fight these battles on our own. The Lord has given us his Holy Spirit to be our advocate and defender against evil. With that kind of power behind us, we can overcome any obstacle on our way to the finish line.

Lord, some days it feels like I can't get to heaven fast enough! Give me strength to fight the good fight of faith. ——

Just for Today: I will push through my own personal "wall."

Healthy Boundaries

*Do you not know that your body is a temple of
the Holy Spirit within you, which you have from God,
and that you are not your own?*

—1 CORINTHIANS 6:19

Making sacrifices, offering our sufferings for another person, and serving the needs of others before our own are all acts of Christian love. However, allowing ourselves to be violated, manipulated, or physically or emotionally abused is not. Maintaining healthy and appropriate boundaries is an essential component of mature Christian charity. If you are involved in a relationship that is destructive or dangerous, or if you are experiencing a repeated violation of your God-given dignity, it is not your Christian duty to remain in harm's way.

There is a vast difference between giving our lives away for another in the name of Christ and engaging in self-destructive, self-abusive behavior that leads to unnecessary suffering. We are called to love one another as ourselves. The essence of this kind of love flows from a respect for and acceptance of our own preciousness in God's sight and the presence of Christ within us. If you are having trouble distinguishing between the two or drawing healthy boundaries, there is help available. You can seek godly counsel from a priest or Catholic social worker or psychologist. Contacting your local Catholic Charities might be a good first step.

Feelings of shame can often keep people from seeking the help they need, but this kind of destructive shame is never of God and is often a threat to authentic Christian love and service. We all endeavor to be good and to live good lives. Our fallen natures make it possible for us to lose sight of our own dignity in the process.

Even as we dedicate ourselves to helping others, we need to tend to our own emotional, physical, and spiritual needs. With God's help, you can experience the peace, safety, security, and personal well-being that come from maintaining healthy, respectful, and firm boundaries in your relationships with others.

Lord, help me to be firm and faithful in my relationships; give me the wisdom and courage I need to build healthy boundaries that are respectful of others and of myself. ⸺

Just for Today: I will make the call to a professional for help if I need it.

He Is Near

Commit your way to the LORD;
trust in him, and he will act.

—PSALM 37:5

I am always amazed that someone as mighty as God would be intimately interested in the smallest detail of our lives. Yet Scripture says that he collects our tears and counts every hair on our heads. What an incredible gift! The same God who created and sustains the universe walks with us each day of our lives and wants to share our most intimate secrets. It is his good pleasure to pour out his love, mercy, and grace into the little cup of our heart and then drink deeply with us every step of the way.

One woman said she believes that God speaks to her, but only from a distant place, and that whatever he might say could only be symbolic or abstract in nature. Her words are not so unusual. In fact, they reflect the way many of us act toward God. We may say that we want a relationship with him; but when it comes right down to it, we don't quite believe that we can actually have one. Yet, there's evidence all around us that God is constantly trying to get our attention, speaking *directly* to our hearts. Through the beauty of nature and especially through the gift of the sacraments, we are invited to experience God's nearness.

One barrier to experiencing a close relationship with God may stem from our tendency to look for God to conform to our own way of thinking. We have a plan for how things ought to be and may even think that we know what God wants in a particular situation. When things don't happen that way, we get discouraged and distrust God. We feel that he is far away from us.

This faulty conclusion gets in the way of our ability to trust and know God more deeply. If we feel that he is far away, it may be because we have not accepted and trusted that his will unfolds in our lives, minute by minute, in a way that is more loving and intimate than we can imagine.

Lord, fill the tiny cup of my heart with a deeper knowledge of you. ⌒

Just for Today: I will listen for the whisper of God's voice in my heart.

The Prudence Prayer

Be quick to hear,
but deliberate in answering.
If you know what to say, answer your neighbor;
but if not, put your hand over your mouth.

—SIRACH 5:11-12

How many times have you wished that you had put your hand over your mouth to keep from speaking? Ten? Twenty? A hundred twenty? Have you ever launched into some sage piece of advice, only to be met with a yawn accompanied by a glassy-eyed stare and an overly polite "thanks for sharing that"? If so, you may have stepped in front of the Holy Spirit in an overzealous yet well-meaning attempt to "speak the truth in love." As wonderful and inspiring as your words may have been, chances are that they weren't prudent for the situation or the person involved.

In fact, prudence in speech is a great grace. It is talked about at length in the Bible. In Ecclesiastes 3:1 we are told that "for everything there is a season, and a time for every matter under heaven." Later on, in verse 7, we are reminded that there is "a time to keep silence, and a time to speak." Oh, such wisdom! We all know too well how much that little tongue of ours can get us into trouble. Conversely, we also know the regret of a missed opportunity to speak up in boldness and truth.

Praying for prudence will ensure that what we say is in line with what needs to be said at any given time. Words are powerful things, so using them with care is a virtue we all need to cultivate.

Lord, let my tongue be an instrument of prudence and compassion and may "the words of my mouth and the meditation of my heart be acceptable to you" (Psalm 19:14). —

Just for Today: I will pray the Prudence Prayer:

Lord, grant me the prudence to keep quiet
    when need be;
courage to speak up only as the Spirit leads me,
and the wisdom to know the difference.
I trust that you alone are the answer and the truth;
you alone are the Word
and will reveal yourself to others,
with or without my help,
in your time and on your terms.
Amen.

Ready or Not

Train children in the right way,
and when old, they will not stray.

—Proverbs 22:6

While trying to navigate through my ten-year-old daughter's room recently, I remembered the times when I used to pick up plastic pails and building blocks along the way. Then it was baby dolls and stuffed animals. Now I'm tangled up in training bras and spending way too much time hunting down my nail polish and perfume under her bed, and I realize that my little girl is growing up. I wonder if I'm really ready for this.

Am I ready for the second round of sleepless nights as I strain to hear her sneaking in past curfew? Am I ready to graduate from tending to skinned knees to mending the first of many broken hearts received from some hapless teenage boy who has stolen the spotlight from her bewildered dad? Am I ready to be looked at as if I am an alien from outer space who is totally clueless when she suddenly discovers that we no longer speak the same language?

No, I don't think I'm ready. Kids grow up too fast these days. What I'm sure of is that no matter what her age, I will always be her mother, and I will be accountable to God for the way that her faith and moral life are formed. If I fulfill my responsibility to give her a firm foundation in Christ and her Catholic faith, then she will be prepared for anything life throws at her.

I think back on all those bedtime prayers we recited in unison, the impromptu "teachable moments" about God, and every rosary we've recited and daily Mass we've attended, and I pray that she has taken them all to heart. I continue to trust in the Lord's provision of safety as she makes her way along the narrow path. I can also trust him to give me the wisdom, counsel, fortitude, and patience required for the job. As a mom-in-training of a soon-to-be-teenage daughter, I'm going to need all the help I can get!

Lord, please give me the grace of a teachable and reachable heart, so that I can be a model for others in the right way to go. ⌐

Just for Today: I will praise God for the seasons of change in my life.

The Gift of Listening

Let everyone be quick to listen.

—James 1:19

"I love listening to their stories!" That was the comment of a teacher who works with seniors who are losing their sight. "I can teach them what to do, but listening to them makes them feel important again, and that's what everybody needs."

This teacher has learned two important truths: that people's stories matter and that there is a need for real listeners in our world today. Seniors are not the only ones who need a listening ear. Children also need our undivided attention, both to model good listening skills and to communicate their preciousness to them. Teenagers need us to listen and validate their deepening insights, and affirm who they are and who they are becoming. Adults need us to listen as they grapple with the complexities of everyday living. They run the risk of skimming the surface of life, never really learning how to listen, even to their own inner voice.

Perhaps the people we listen to the least are the ones with whom we spend the most time: our spouse, our children, our parents. This lack of listening can become a constant undercurrent of contention and strife in the home, without our ever really acknowledging it. I wonder how many problems in families could be solved or arguments avoided if we really stopped to listen from the heart to the person who is speaking to us. Our attention is a gift we give to one another. Taking time to listen from the heart will truly make a difference, not just for the ones we are listening to, but for us as well.

When we listen from the heart, we experience a deeper connection with others. When we resist the temptation to offer our advice or make a clever remark, we can relax and enjoy our conversations and validate the people in our lives. In a sense, we become what St. Teresa Benedicta of the Cross described as "persons who are used as instruments to awaken and nurture the divine spark."[13] Ultimately, the gift of listening goes both ways. Take time to listen, and see what you receive in return.

Lord, settle my soul, and give me a listening heart. ⸺

Just for Today: I will seize the opportunity to give the gift of my undivided attention to someone in my family.

Faith Walk

The human mind plans the way,
but the LORD directs the steps.

—PROVERBS 16:9

God can seem elusive sometimes. At difficult crossroads in our lives, we may ask God to give us direction, only to be met with silence and a wide-open road before us. It may feel as though we are traveling all alone and that God is either unconcerned or unwilling to help us determine the next destination on our path.

Though we may experience feelings of uncertainty, confusion, or anxiety about what to do next, God is present with us even at these crossroads. We can be comforted by the fact that God is not off in the distance like a stern traffic cop, ready to "issue a ticket" if we make a misstep or go the wrong way down a one-way ramp. He is more like a wise but unobtrusive tour guide who is familiar with the territory we are about to cover and can help us get back on track if we make a wrong turn.

We can consult our compassionate companion every step of the way, knowing that it is God's desire to guide and accompany us on our journey. He wants us to get the most out of the scenery and enjoy each experience along the way. When we are confounded by choices or lack of them, when it comes to which direction to take, we are called to commit to a path and take the first step of faith.

With those uncertain steps, God honors our best attempts toward obedience and is pleased when we trust in him. The truth is that he doesn't always let us know the best route or the right road to take. He leaves it up to our own free will and discernment, but he never abandons us. Maybe more important than the question of "Which way should I go?" is "How am I being called to proceed from here?"—even without being completely clear about what lies ahead. This is the faith walk, and it can only begin when we are willing to take that first step.

Lord, help me trust in your guidance, even when I cannot make sense of the direction of my life. —

Just for Today: I will take one small step of faith.

Modern-Day Martha

*"You are worried and distracted by many things;
there is need of only one thing."*

—LUKE 10:41-42

In an informal survey, twenty women were asked to describe their lives in just one word. Over half of them said, "Busy!" Our age or stage of life doesn't seem to matter; the common denominator is that we are all rushing around in an effort to get things done.

Maybe it's because people today have so many activities. And when we multiply those activities by the number of people we are responsible for, life can get pretty complicated. In nearly every culture, women have been the organizers and managers of time within the family. We see from the story of Martha and Mary that even in biblical times, the women were expected to "run the show" within the household.

We modern-day Marthas are "dancing as fast as we can"—more out of necessity than choice. And like Martha, who among us hasn't looked up to God and pleaded, "Lord, don't you care that I am doing all the work?" Of course, he cares. However, I am quite sure that Jesus would give us the same answer he gave to his beloved friend two thousand years ago.

Jesus is telling us, just as he told Martha, that the "one thing" we need is him. When we put him first in line for our attention, our time, and our energy, the "busyness" of our days becomes more purposeful, less hectic, and more enjoyable. This is an amazing spiritual paradox: the more time we give to Jesus, the more time we have to give. It's the same multiplication principle that fed thousands with just two loaves and five fish. So the next time you have two hours and fifteen different tasks to accomplish, take time to put Jesus first. You'll be amazed at the results!

Lord, help me to slow down and put you first throughout my day. I need your guidance to get things done, and I am grateful for your companionship— even when I'm too busy to notice! —

Just for Today: I will stop what I am doing and spend a moment thanking Jesus for his help and presence in my life.

No More Worries

"Can any of you by worrying add a single hour to your span of life? If then you are not able to do so small a thing as that, why do you worry about the rest?"

—LUKE 12:25-26

"Worry never works!" Those were the words of a wise and wonderful friend of mine, as I shared with her what seemed like an impossible situation one day. "You can't apply worry to a situation and expect it to be solved, any more than you can apply salt to a wound to make it better," she said. It made a lot of sense when she put it that way.

Pondering her words, I realized that I was devoting more energy to worrying than to working out a solution. It was as if I thought that worrying about the problem long enough might make it go away. Once I decided that worry was wasting my time and wasn't going to get me any closer to an answer, my thoughts began to clear, and I began to move toward a decision that would lead to a resolution.

Worrying might be a useful first step in recognizing that something is wrong, but we can't get stuck there. Sometimes we get tricked into thinking that worrying is a form of helping. Our prayers may even become just a rehashing and restating of our fears and anxieties, never progressing to the next step of empowerment and action in the Spirit of God.

If the evil one can keep us wrapped up in our worries, then he can keep us hiding in the darkness, plagued by problems that seem insurmountable. Jesus said, however, "My yoke is easy, and my burden is light" (Matthew 11:30). Clearly, we will have burdens in our lives. But if we allow our thoughts, concerns, and actions to come under the gentle yoke of Christ, we will have the energy and inspiration to confront our worries and work them out together with Christ for the good of others and ourselves.

Lord, help me to resist the temptation to worry. Let me trust in you instead. ⟶

Just for Today: I will put all my energy into trusting Jesus.

In His Presence

Immediately aware that power had gone forth from him,
Jesus turned about in the crowd and said,
"Who touched my clothes?"

—MARK 5:30

If we know anything about Jesus, it's that he is approachable. The Scriptures tell us of many people who went to great lengths to be in his presence. The Syrophoenician woman burst into the home of a complete stranger to sit at his feet, and four men labored to cut through a roof so that their paralyzed friend could be healed. There were children who persisted, as only children can, to have a few moments by his side. And of course, there was the suffering woman who crawled on the ground, expecting miracles from the mere touch of Jesus' cloak.

When Jesus said, "Foxes have holes, and birds of the air have nests; but the Son of Man has nowhere to lay his head" (Matthew 8:20), he was referring to himself, but he could have also been talking about the lives of women in the twenty-first century! How many of us have experienced days (maybe weeks) when from sunup to sundown we were surrounded by people clamoring for our attention? It could be our children, our co-workers, our husband, our mother, or all of the above. But just like Jesus, we sometimes feel as if we have no place to lay our heads, as we tackle the nonstop needs of our loved ones. We feel as if we have little time to think about whether we are approachable or not or how we might be responding to the people around us. Let today be different.

Instead of jumping out of bed to tackle the first of your many duties, take a moment to think about how you could communicate your approachability to others. Reflect on one of the stories mentioned above and focus on the Lord's response. Imagine how he might have ministered to people in the midst of the chaotic crowds. Think of how you can imitate his approachability with your own personality and style. When you do, you might find that no matter what the circumstances, you can be enriched by your encounters with others, instead of being exhausted by them. Jesus will be right there with you to give you the graces you need to get through another hectic day.

Lord, help me to be more open and approachable to those around me today. —

Just for Today: I will be approachable in my own home.

Simple Staircase

When you turn to the right or when you turn to the left,
your ears shall hear a word behind you, saying,
"This is the way; walk in it."

—ISAIAH 30:21

The straightest path to God is via the simple staircase of our daily duties.

The staircase is a symbol for the "one foot in front of the other" form of spirituality, which applies practicality to the spiritual journey. Sometimes we become impatient with ourselves and try to take several steps at a time, only to stumble over our own pride in the process.

If you've ever climbed the narrow steps to the top of a lighthouse, you'll remember that its spiral structure causes the climber to place her focus, not on the distant destination, but on the very next step, so that she doesn't get dizzy or disoriented. Step after dutiful step, one seemingly identical to the next, the climber keeps on going until she finally reaches the open platform at the top that's filled with light, activity, and a marvelous view.

St. Thérèse of Lisieux described the spiritual life in terms of a little child trying to climb the stairs. He keeps trying but just can't get past the first step. The child needs the help of his mother or father, just as we need the help of the Lord. We can ask God to help us along the way by stripping away any spiritual distraction in our lives and by helping us to focus on whatever needs to be done that is right in front of us each day. A loving smile, a load of laundry, or a little restraint in a conversation at work are all examples of the tiny steps that lead us further up the staircase of spiritual growth and closeness to the Lord.

We know where we are headed, and just imagining the beautiful view that awaits us can keep us climbing. No matter how steep the steps along the way, we can trust that the Light at the end of our journey will welcome us with open arms.

Lord, help me to stay on track and to keep my feet firmly planted on your chosen path for me. Let your word be a "lamp to my feet / and a light to my path" (Psalm 119:105) as I journey through this life back to you. ⸺

Just for Today: I will thank God for the simple staircase of my own spiritual walk.

His Heart's Work

"The harvest is plentiful, but the laborers are few."

—MATTHEW 9:37

God's goodness makes each moment a consecrated gift, and his love constantly brings purification and, through Jesus, salvation for souls. God's loving action in the world continuously creates and cleanses, and each soul is his unrepeatable "project," his heart's work.

One way to envision God is as a tender and humble laborer. His love toils for the sake of every single soul. He is eternally willing to "get his hands dirty" as a working God whose heart contains the entire universe. Think of God as a loving gardener who "digs in" and sweats it out with every single seed of life he has planted. We, as Christians and his children, are his apprentices. We are called to be laborers in the field and are commanded to stay busy before the harvest. Just as St. Paul describes us all as members of the body of Christ, we each have a distinct function and duty to get in there and roll up our sleeves with God to nurture the budding blossom or prune the stubborn branch. In other words, we are responsible, as long as we are here, for the condition of the fields and the souls that are planted here.

Yes, God is at work all the time, and we can't fall down on the job now. The long evening has begun, and soon it will be night. The harvest will be ready, and God is counting on us. We cannot get discouraged by what seems like an impossible tangle of debris or an uncontrollable patch of weeds. God isn't. He sees the glory of the promised harvest, and he knows that it is good.

If God is willing to work, then we ought to be willing to struggle and stretch ourselves to the limits for souls that are lost. We can offer prayers and sacrifice. We can evangelize through our daily actions. This is the work of the Christian life, and we look forward to completing it, so that we too can partake of the bounty that is yet to come.

Lord, I am grateful for the Father's example of active love for every soul. Help me to never tire of the work of saving souls for the harvest. —

Just for Today: I will act in some way on behalf of another soul.

A New Creation

If anyone is in Christ, there is a new creation:
everything old has passed away.

—2 CORINTHIANS 5:17

We are all called to serve. In our world today, we can get hung up on status or the glory of our achievements, career, or education. But service doesn't have anything to do with these things. The quality of our service to others does not depend on what we know. Rather, it is essentially the fruit of a humble heart.

Jesus said that to gain life, we must lose it. He didn't say that we had to produce good results or get a degree first. We lose our lives in service to others when we embrace the spiritual freedom that comes from putting ourselves last. At first it is a difficult discipline, because our fallen nature is much more concerned with self than others. Yet the *Catechism of the Catholic Church* reminds us that by virtue of our "baptism we are not only purified of our sins, but we are made into a new creature . . . a partaker of the divine nature" (1265).

One new mother remarked that she never knew how selfish she was until she had a child. Suddenly everything that used to be important in her life was put on the back burner so that she could devote every waking hour (and some hours when she wasn't quite awake!) to caring for her bundle of joy. Even as she loved that little one with every ounce of her being and willingly gave up her former life and freedoms, she admitted that it didn't come naturally, nor was it always an easy choice.

With practice, and by calling on God's grace as we exercise the spiritual muscle of self-sacrifice, we can embrace a "new nature" and become more like Christ, who was selfless unto death. Dr. Martin Luther King, Jr., once said, "Everybody can be great because anybody can serve. You don't have to have a college degree. You don't have to make your subject and verb agree to serve. You only need a heart full of grace. A soul generated by love."[14]

Sweet Jesus, let it be so. ⟶

Just for Today: I will seek a "heart full of grace" and a "soul generated by love."

New Freedom

Now the Lord is the Spirit, and where the Spirit of the Lord is, there is freedom.

—2 CORINTHIANS 3:17

Sometimes life can bog us down. We start the day refreshed and ready for anything, only to end it with an eroded sense of enthusiasm and a heavy dose of exhaustion. We may have the best of intentions, but the rigors of life can wear on us. We even begin to blame ourselves when things don't turn out the way we had hoped. For example, one mother who was having significant difficulty relating to one of her children came to the faulty conclusion that she was a failure as a mother.

In these situations, the Holy Spirit can give us a fresh breath of freedom—if we only let him. No matter how bad or overwhelmed we may feel inside, we can invite the Holy Spirit to "create in [us] a clean heart [and mind] . . . / and put a new and right spirit within [us]." There is power in these words from Psalm 51:10. Taking them to heart can release a renewal within us and loosen the bonds of inner negativity and confusion that result from emotional exhaustion of any sort.

One of our greatest challenges in life is to learn how to honor the rhythms and callings of our own souls. Before we can "breathe freely" again, we need to stop and reflect. This pause will enable us to recognize our wrong turns and worn-out ways of relating to others and ourselves.

Trusting in God's mercy and in the goodness of his path will guard us from becoming discouraged and help us resist the temptation to condemn ourselves for our limitations. If we are in bondage to something, it is not because we are bad; we are merely human. When we cooperate with God's grace and call on the Holy Spirit to activate our wisdom, intelligence, energy, and purpose, something very beautiful happens. Our lives become a new symphony of freedom and frailties, full of depth and meaning, completely in tune with God's infinite love.

Lord, create in me a new heart and put a right spirit within me. ⟶

Just for Today: I will reflect on the ways in which I am bound and be open to new ways of freedom from the Holy Spirit.

Original Beauty

Wash me thoroughly from my iniquity,
and cleanse me from my sin.

—Psalm 51:2

When I was a child, I was fascinated by a TV commercial touting a "revolutionary" product that could restore old, tarnished silver pieces to their original luster almost instantly. Whether it was a serving platter or a spotty old coin, the part of the object that was dipped into the "magic" liquid came out sparkling like new. I begged my mother for the product in spite of her warnings that it wasn't as easy as it looked.

Dying to find out the truth, I remember my excitement as I sat in our kitchen, armed with our silver and the coveted liquid. Guess what? The pieces came out as tarnished as they were when they were put in. I soon discovered that the only way to get the shine back was to apply some old-fashioned elbow grease. Deflated, I went about polishing the silver slowly and meticulously, scrubbing and buffing until every crevice and groove was coaxed into its former grandeur. Back then I didn't see any deep spiritual message in the whole affair, but I do now.

This lesson in restoration reminds me that even as God sees the beauty and sparkle of our souls beneath the stain of our sins, we have to put forth effort to cooperate with his grace as we are cleansed. Through our baptism, we are wiped clean—not because of any magic potion, but because of the sacrifice of Jesus. Throughout our lives, the Sacrament of Reconciliation restores us to our original state of grace. Christ died once and for all for our sins, but we are still called to apply our wills to make amends for our failings.

The *Catechism of the Catholic Church* says that "the sinner must still recover his full spiritual health by doing something more to make amends for the sin; he must 'make satisfaction for' or 'expiate' his sins" (1459). With God's grace, may we be willing to apply the spiritual elbow grease that is needed to completely wipe away the stain of our sins in order to be restored by God to our original beauty.

Father, lead me away from quick fixes and the temptation to gloss over my sins. Restore me in mind, heart, and soul. ⸻

Just for Today: I will remember that God longs to restore me in his good grace, and I will prepare for a good confession.

A Shepherd's Voice

"He calls his own sheep by name . . . and the sheep follow him because they know his voice."

—JOHN 10:3-4

It is said that a mother can distinguish the cries of her newborn from those of others in a nursery when the child is just hours old. Likewise, studies have shown that newborns know the sound of their parents' voices from almost the time of their birth. This speaks to the deep spiritual and emotional bond between parents and their children. Deeper still is the bond between the Good Shepherd and his sheep.

Have you ever heard Jesus call your name? Not necessarily in an audible way, but maybe in the depths of your heart? Perhaps there was a time when you knew that Jesus was with you as you were going through a personal crisis. Or perhaps you were certain that he sent an angel in the form of another human being to let you know that he was near. We experience these times of closeness because Jesus wants to communicate with us on a very intimate level.

We talk with many people every day, but only on a superficial level, using speech in a functional way to explain, to get things done, and to keep our lives running smoothly. The Shepherd, on the other hand, desires to communicate through a language that transcends functionality and plunges into the deep waters of our hearts. This is the realm of intimate connection. Jesus longs for us to take the time to listen, so that we can distinguish his voice and learn more about his love.

To meet Jesus at this level, we need to listen for his knock and open the doors of our hearts. This may mean that in the middle of our errands, we stop to enjoy a moment of solitude or spend five minutes contemplating the crucifix. We may spend the lunch hour before the Blessed Sacrament or take a few moments to write a prayer to God in a journal. Our efforts will not fall on deaf ears, for the Shepherd is always listening and always ready to respond to the needs of his beloved sheep.

Lord, give me the grace to hear you through the busyness and noise of my life. I long to connect with you as you speak your language of love into my life. ⁓

Just for Today: I will quiet my heart and listen for the words Jesus wants me to hear.

Miracle of Plenty

*And taking the five loaves and the two fish, he looked up
to heaven, and blessed and broke them, and gave them
to the disciples to set before the crowd.
And all ate and were filled.*

—LUKE 9:16-17

The story of the loaves and fishes is a fascinating one. It is the only one of Jesus' miracles that is recounted in all four gospels of the New Testament, and it is one of the most widely known of the multiplication miracles. What makes it especially interesting is the way Jesus chose to engage the disciples in the process. He knew what little rations they had, but he asked them for a contribution, nonetheless. The two fish and few loaves were totally inadequate to feed the crowd, but Jesus didn't focus on that. The important thing was that the disciples offered what they had back to him to meet the enormous need of the crowd.

The story mirrors our own situation. What we possess on our own will never be enough to meet the needs of others. When we trust enough to turn our gifts, talents, desires, hopes, dreams, and "doings" over to Jesus, he will multiply them and more than meet the needs that are before us. If you are a mother who has only a smidgen of patience left or a daughter who is completely out of energy in caring for a parent with dementia, or if you are teacher who is overwhelmed by the needs of your students—no matter what your circumstances, remember that Jesus *is* enough. He will give you what you need to meet the demand. And he will provide not only what you *need*, but an abundance—one that leaves twelve baskets full!

It's a principle that you can count on, so don't delay in offering up to the Lord what little you have. Our insufficiency is always met by God's all-sufficiency. The multiplication miracle is just as possible today as it was when Jesus walked the earth, so whatever "hungry crowd" confronts you, turn it over to the Lord. Then he can use you as an instrument of his abundance by providing what you need, and more!

Lord, I give you everything I have. Please work a miracle of plenty in my life. ⟶

Just for Today: I will make a list of my gifts and talents and place it at the foot of a crucifix.

Making Peace with the Past

Do not fear, for you will not be ashamed;
do not be discouraged, for you will not suffer disgrace;
for you will forget the shame of your youth.

—Isaiah 54:4

There's a saying that even God can't change the past. Whether he can or not, we know for certain that God *doesn't* change the past, and with good reason. There's too much for us to learn from our personal experiences and pasts to change them. The lifelong process of making peace with our past—whether it's the temper tantrum we threw yesterday or the wrong turns we took as teenagers—is vital to developing a strong and trusting relationship with God.

Especially when we are having difficulty moving on, the advice "Don't dwell in the past" may not be very useful, because wiping away painful memories is not as simple as waving a mental magic wand. If we have regrets or carry guilt with us because of a decision we made or failed to make, we can do something today to put the past in perspective.

The first step is to recognize that we are different people today than we were in the past. We benefit from living life day by day, and even though it may seem like we never change, we do. We grow and mature simply by living, and with living comes greater knowledge of ourselves and of others.

Second, we need to honor our past for what it was. Our journey toward acceptance requires us to have the courage to acknowledge the truth of our past, even if it was painful or stirs up authentic or undeserved shame. Facing the truth of our past will set us free. We can only do this with the help of the Holy Spirit, who will provide guidance and clarity to enable us to trust our memories, feel our feelings, and ultimately put our pasts behind us. Going to the Sacrament of Reconciliation for any unconfessed sins will place a seal of mercy on our past and enable us to embrace the transforming future God has for us right now.

Lord, guide me as I make peace with my past. Enlighten my mind and lift my heart to receive your mercy and love today. ⸺

Just for Today: I will forgive myself for any past mistakes and failures.

Vive la Différence!

May the God of steadfastness and encouragement grant
you to live in harmony with one another.

—ROMANS 15:5

Science has revealed that a woman's brain is uniquely equipped to do more than one thing at a time without even thinking about it.[15] In other words, our brains are biologically programmed to multitask. We can cook dinner, talk on the phone, plan a meeting, do laundry, and make sure our kids are doing their homework, all at the same time. It just comes naturally to us!

The men in our lives, on the other hand, are much more focused and honed in on the one thing that is right in front of them. Whether it is the NBA play-offs, the latest stock market quotes, or the car they are fixing, most men will be completely absorbed in the task and unable to do other things simultaneously, such as carry on a conversation or even realize that someone else is in the room! This ability to hyper-focus comes in handy for their roles as protector and provider. The human male, whether the hunter-gatherer of civilizations past or the corporate executive of today, is designed to direct all of his energy and attention to get the job done, not just for himself, but for his family.

While research helps to explain and understand the differences between men and women, our faith assures us that God intended it this way. By design we are not made to be identical to men, but to be complementary to them. There is a need for both male and female brains in the world. Though some days it might really get on our nerves, our distinct abilities and ways of looking at the world are necessary for the roles we play throughout our lives.

The next time you find yourself getting frustrated with the beloved male in your life as the tasks pile up around you, remember to compliment him on his unique ability to focus on one thing at a time, and thank him for it. A kind word of appreciation will help to change your perspective, and it might even get him to notice the next thing on the to-do list!

Lord, thank you for the differences between the men in my life and me. ⎯

Just for Today: I will show my appreciation for the differences of others.

The Gift of Tears

Those who go out weeping,
bearing the seed for sowing,
shall come home with shouts of joy,
carrying their sheaves.

—Psalm 126:6

One of the greatest gifts we can give to others is to help them understand and express the gift of their tears. One of the shortest sentences in the Bible and perhaps the most powerful is "Jesus began to weep" (John 11:35). That image of our perfect savior shedding tears of sorrow at the death of his beloved friend Lazarus shows us how important it is to express our emotions freely and unashamedly. What an amazing reality! God cries, too.

It's important to cry, because tears are as much a part of our physical, emotional, and spiritual well-being as any form of exercise, drug, or therapeutic intervention. Tears cleanse the body and spirit. Psalm 51:10 pleads, "Create in me a clean heart, O God, / and put a new and right spirit within me." God cleans our hearts, in part, through our tears.

People often equate tears with weakness, but tears are essential to our overall strength of mind and body.

If we are afraid, our tears bring courage. If we are brokenhearted and filled with sorrow, the flow of our tears is the first step back toward wholeness and joy. Our true strength lies in the authentic expression of our feelings. Helping others to honor the truth of their feelings can set them on a path to emotional freedom and self-acceptance.

For many of us, the message "Don't cry!" or "Stop crying!" has been ingrained in us from when we were very young, because our tears made someone else uncomfortable. As a result, we learned to cut ourselves off from the source of our tears. Far from making us strong, this disconnection can weaken us emotionally and may even cause physical distress and disease. Giving others permission to cry in our presence is a profound act of love. Showing them through our acceptance that their tears are a gift may help them to be more loving and accepting of themselves. And the free flow of their tears is likely to make them healthier in mind, body, and spirit.

Lord, help me to receive the gift of my tears and those of others. Help me to honor my deepest feelings and empower others to express theirs also. ⟶

Just for Today: I will honor the tears of another.

Forgiving First

"Whenever you stand praying, forgive, if you have
anything against anyone; so that your Father in heaven
may also forgive you."

—MARK 11:25

Our faith tells us that a giving heart must also be a heart
that forgives. We can't hold on to hurts, grudges, bitterness, or anger toward others and expect to be able to
love as Christ does. In the garden of Gethsemane, even
though Jesus knew that Judas had betrayed him, Jesus
still called him friend. Even as our Lord was giving his
life to save us on the cross, he forgave those who "do
not know what they are doing" (Luke 23:34).

What about those who *do* know what they are
doing? What about those people who keep hurting us,
or who don't show any signs of remorse or even seem
to want our forgiveness? What do we do then? Jesus
answered these questions when Peter asked him, "Lord,
if another member of the church sins against me, how
often should I forgive? As many as seven times?" Peter
had some inkling that we should be generous with our
forgiveness, but Jesus replied, "Not seven times, but, I
tell you, seventy-seven times" (Matthew 18:21-22).

Jesus didn't expect us to be capable of this over-the-top forgiveness on our own. We need him to accomplish it. We need his grace to wrestle ourselves free from the heavy weight of anger, hurt, and resentment within us. "God, be merciful to me, a sinner" (Luke 18:13). That short prayer is our first step toward forgiveness. As we become willing to receive God's mercy and forgiveness for ourselves, we will become capable of showing mercy and forgiveness to others.

It's good to check in with what's going on in our hearts from time to time. Taking a quiet inventory of what grudges or resentments we are holding on to will help us to evaluate our "heart condition." If we find that we need to forgive, then the prescription is to stop what we are doing and pray for the grace to begin the work of forgiveness.

Lord, your examples of forgiveness inspire me. Give me the grace to forgive those who have hurt me. ⌣

Just for Today: I will take an inventory to determine the condition of my heart.

One Better

> *"For I have set you an example, that you also should do as I have done to you."*
>
> —JOHN 13:15

The manager of a small Catholic radio station was asked at his retirement party to reflect on his life's work and sum it up in ten words or less. "I've just treated people better than I treat myself," he replied humbly. It was a simple but accurate response for a life well lived and a job well done.

This way of living seems to go one step further than treating others as we want to be treated. Instead, it calls for treating them *better* than we want to be treated. This is certainly in keeping with the spirit of Christ's greatest commandment, and it is a reflection of how Jesus lived his life. When we elevate others and treat them with the utmost dignity and respect, we are embracing the example Christ left us when he shared his last meal with his disciples and washed their feet.

Jean Vanier, the founder of L'Arche communities, explored the profound meaning of Jesus' humble act of service—which is the only place in the gospels where Jesus gives us a direct example to follow. What makes this act so significant, Vanier notes, is that "as Jesus humbly kneels before each of his disciples and washes their feet, he forgives them *from below*."[16] This is God taking "second place" and raising up his human friends, cleansing them with his mercy and love. What a model Jesus offers for treating others better than we treat ourselves!

At Mass, when Christ comes to us in the Eucharist and we recall his humble sacrifice for the forgiveness of our sins, let us remember the example we are called to embrace. Essentially, we are to love from behind, to give from below, and to elevate others, putting their needs before our own. In turn, Jesus will lift up our hearts and minds to be nourished by him for a life of self-forgetfulness and service in his name, and there's really nothing better than that!

Heavenly Father, let my actions throughout the day communicate to others their value, dignity, and worth. ——

Just for Today: I will treat someone better than I treat myself.

A Little Miracle

Let each of you look not to your own interests,
but to the interests of others.

—PHILIPPIANS 2:4

On Christmas Eve in 1886, a thirteen-year-old girl received a great gift. She was, by all accounts, an overly sensitive girl. She carried on at the slightest provocation, to the point of being irksome to those around her, namely her sisters and her beloved father. She described herself in later years as a "very great trial to others," but she found herself "powerless to correct the fault" and in great need of "a miracle to make her grow up once and for all."

That miracle came after midnight Mass, in her response to a comment she had overheard from her father. He was bemoaning the fact that he still had to prepare gifts and place them in her shoe, as was the custom of the day. His words cut into the sensitive girl's heart. She was horrified to discover that she was a burden to the one she loved the most. However, instead of reacting the way she usually would have, with a tearful tantrum, she did something quite extraordinary. She put on a happy face, acted as though she had never heard her father's words, and gratefully opened the presents, never mentioning another word about it.

Although St. Thérèse of Lisieux had spent many years of her life working unsuccessfully to change herself, the Lord completed the job in an instant. Describing the incident as an adult, she wrote, "I felt charity enter into my soul, and the need to forget myself and please others; since then I've been happy."[17]

It seems paradoxical that the only way to experience sustained happiness in life is to forget our own needs. But when we remove ourselves from the center of our attention, God has room to step in. How many parents have looked at their children and thought, "I only want my child to be happy"? We can ensure their happiness by teaching the lesson of self-forgetfulness so that charity for others can take root in their hearts.

Lord, give me your grace to model selflessness in my dealings with others. —

Just for Today: I will forget an offense made against me.

Personal Vocation

Lead a life worthy of the calling to which you have been called. . . . Each of us was given grace according to the measure of Christ's gift.

—EPHESIANS 4 : 1 , 7

We so often think of vocation as something that we do or accomplish—an action, as opposed to a commitment. However, vocation in its fullest sense is not what we do but who we are—and who we become—in Christ. It is our heart's commitment to God's presence within us. Therefore, each one of us has a vocation, a deep meaning, and a unique purpose in the body of Christ. Our relationship with Jesus and our acceptance of his uniquely chosen gifts for our lives determine the extent to which we express our vocation on a daily basis.

Author Herbert Alphonso, SJ, describes personal vocation as "the unique and unrepeatable God-given meaning in a person's life." For example, while ten or a hundred people may discern a call to service in their lives, each one will have his or her own personal way of being a servant. This way will be completely unique and unchangeable for that person on the spiritual level. As Alphonso explains, "Every single one of us has, in our personal vocation, our own unique way of giving and surrendering self in any human experience."[18]

We should take time to reflect on our personal vocations as they relate to who we are as women in our families, friendship circles, churches, and society at large. How do God's dreams for us fit in? Who are we being called to become? How does the pace of our lives enhance or detract from discerning our personal vocations? However we express our personal vocation, it will surely draw us deeper into the heart of God. We can trust that as our lives unfold, he will continually affirm us and teach us more about ourselves and his heart in the process.

Heavenly Father, help me to embrace all that is unique within me, and show me the way to express my vocation more deeply. —

Just for Today: I will take a few moments to ponder the reality of what it means to be created in God's image and thank him for calling me to my present vocation.

God Knows

*Trust in the LORD with all your heart,
and do not rely on your own insight.*

—PROVERBS 3:5

Why did the woman who so desperately wanted to have a child lose her daughter within hours of her birth? Why did the teenage boy lose control of his car, ending a life that had barely begun? Why did my best friend choose to take her own life, leaving us all to grapple with the mystery of her personal darkness? Why? Why? *Why?*

Tragedy never makes sense. In the aftermath of searing pain and confusion, the open wound of suffering can become infected with the need to know why. Among those of us who have endured tragedy, the fortunate ones have learned to "live" their questions. They have taken the advice of Rainer Maria Rilke, who wrote in *Letters to a Young Poet,*

> Have patience with everything unresolved in your heart and try to love the questions themselves. . . . Don't search for the answers, which could not be given to you now, because you would not be able to live them. And the point is, to live everything.

. . . Perhaps then, someday far in the future, you will gradually, without even noticing it, live your way into the answer.[19]

There is no greater form of self-surrender than letting go of the need to have answers to the unanswerable questions in life. Freedom comes, and life begins again, when we release ourselves from the need to know the unknowable. Or maybe it is God himself who gives us the grace to let go. The doctor must learn to stop asking, "Why can't I find the source of the pain?" The mother, "Why couldn't I save this child?" And the friend must let go of the need to know, "Why couldn't I save her from her suffering?"

God instructs us not to lean on our own understanding, because it will never be enough. Instead, we can offer our "not knowing" as a prayer from the depth of our hearts. With God's grace, we will reach the plateau of peace, where all we need to know is that God knows, and that is good enough for us to carry on.

Lord, give me the grace to live with my questions and trust in your all-knowing love. ⎯

Just for Today: I will make peace with my questions and hold on to hope in my heart.

Whom Can We Trust?

Trust in the LORD forever,
for in the LORD GOD
you have an everlasting rock.

—ISAIAH 26:4

Trust is an issue for many of us, even though we were not created by God to mistrust. Quite the contrary, in fact, for an infant can do nothing but place her full trust in the benevolence of her caregivers. But as we journey through life, broken promises, real or imagined betrayal, and the harsh consequences of living in a fallen world erode our trust. As a result, we are left to grapple with our feelings of insecurity, confusion, and doubt.

A wise saying advises us to "trust God and love people," because we know that people are imperfect. Still, we love them and thus take a risk each time we do, knowing they have the capacity to violate our trust and let us down. It's easier for us to do this when we remember that we are imperfect also and have the capacity to let others down, as well.

God, on the other hand, is completely trustworthy. The cornerstone of his nature is that he is unchanging and unfailing. We can completely count on him. Did you know that trust is the topic of more than 150 Bible passages? Most of them extol the benefits of trusting in the Lord for all of our needs. So why is that so hard for us to do?

Maybe it's because we don't really know God all that well. Trust is only possible in relationships in which a certain level of intimacy has been established. Put simply, to know God better, we need to seek him. One place to find him is in the Scriptures. From them we can learn that God is all good and all loving (see Luke 18:19; Psalm 25:10); God is on our side (see Romans 8:31); God knows and accepts us (see Psalm 139); God delights in us (see Psalm 37:23); all things will "work together for good" for those who love God (see Romans 8:28); God has an eternal plan for our happiness (see Jeremiah 29:11); God is always listening (see Psalm 10:17); and God will never reject us (see 1 Timothy 4:4).

And there's so much more!

Father God, teach me your ways, and help me to trust in you always! ⌒

Just for Today: I will seek God by reading the Bible (especially the psalms).

Poverty in Prayer

Pray in the Spirit at all times in every prayer
and supplication.

—Ephesians 6:18

Janet is a true prayer warrior. She is the "go-to gal" in our women's group for any and every prayer need that is on the hearts of those in our parish. While many people participate in the prayer chain, Janet is one of the few able to devote not just a few minutes but many hours to prayer for others, and she usually does just that.

It seems that anyone who calls or drops by finds that Janet was "just offering up a little prayer." Sometimes it is as simple as a prayer for her niece to pass a spelling test, while another day it could be as dire as the need for a miracle to stop a growing tumor. Each prayer gets the same amount of "praying time" from Janet. Her trust in the Lord's provision seems to grow stronger with every intercessory prayer she offers, whether the prayers are answered or not. While others get discouraged by "unanswered" prayers, Janet seems all the more determined in her prayer life—thus the label of "warrior," which truly fits this dedicated woman of faith.

Seen as a prayer "veteran" by the younger women in our church, Janet was asked to share the secret of her prayer life with others over tea. Clearly uncomfortable with "all the fuss," Janet confessed that her most effective times of prayer were the ones when she said virtually nothing at all. "Sometimes I just bring people to the altar and leave them there," she explained. "I have no idea what to say, but I know that God knows what to do with them. I carry them there with my prayers, but God does all the work!"

Janet has no secret formula or special hotline to God, just an incredibly simple faith that focuses more on her relationship with Christ than on the results of her prayers. For every prayer request, she simply empties her heart before Christ and trusts in his loving response to the needs she presents. In this way, we can all be prayer warriors. We can be women of tenacious trust with rich prayer lives if we will surrender to God's goodness and leave the results to him.

Lord, deepen my faith and relationship with you through my prayer life. ⟶

Just for Today: Pray through the silence, and seek the Lord's intentions for those who are in your heart today.

Keeping It Simple

The LORD protects the simple;
when I was brought low, he saved me.
Return, O my soul, to your rest,
for the LORD has dealt bountifully with you.

—PSALM 116:6-7

There probably isn't a woman alive who wouldn't agree with the following: "Year by year the complexities of this world become more bewildering and so each year we need all the more to seek peace and comfort in the joyful simplistics." However, this statement didn't come from a book on today's best-seller list; it was taken from a 1935 edition of *The Woman's Home Companion*![20]

It's eye opening to learn that the generations of women before us—our mothers and grandmothers—confronted some of the same challenges we face today. How did they cope? Clearly, their lives weren't crammed with as many choices and distractions as ours. But each generation is faced with the dilemma of "progress" and the complexity that comes with it.

Even when we have a million things to do each day, we can still simplify our lives. Simplicity has just as much to do with purifying our hearts and lives as it does with pruning them of excess activities. For instance, we can spend fifteen minutes reading a book to a child, or we can spend them chatting with the neighbor about the latest gossip on the block. We can spend half an hour saying the rosary or spend it surfing the Internet. We can contemplate a sunset or watch a sitcom. We can go to the casino or go to the woods. It's all a matter of how, on what, and where we focus our attention. Simplicity, peace, and comfort come from the depth and meaning we give to and receive from our activities each day. It is not how much we experience in our lives, but the quality of the life experience, that will bring us back to simplicity and purity.

Many busy and productive people live very simple lives. Mother Teresa comes to mind, for one. Her heart's priorities were set on the Lord, and her attention was focused on the things that mattered most. We can do the same and, in turn, be models for the next generations of women to come.

Lord, help me to keep it simple. —

Just for Today: I will seek out a quality experience that will bring comfort to me or someone else.

Speaking of Salt

Let your speech always be gracious, seasoned with salt, so that you may know how you ought to answer everyone.

—COLOSSIANS 4:6

Have you ever known someone who always tells you exactly what you want to hear? It's almost a given that you won't really trust that person, because no two people can be so closely knit that they are in full agreement all the time.

Colossians 4:6 reinforces the value of being charitable in our speech. Yet as Christians, we are also called to do something far more difficult and meaningful: we are called to speak the truth in love.

Sometimes salt can be an irritant. It can also sting when applied, but it will always be "cleansing" in its application. When our words are "seasoned with salt," we bring clarity to a situation. We preserve ourselves from selling out to the common denominator of culture and from using our speech to harm or manipulate. Salt will sometimes alienate us from others, but it can also heal the hurts of those who have been lied to or who are seeking authentic truth and the trustworthiness of someone who will speak it.

We always have a choice to make when it comes to how we "answer everyone."

To the best of our ability, we need to strive for speech that is Spirit driven. There is a big difference between rubbing salt in a wound and seasoning our speech with salt, much like the difference between bluntness and boldness. The former has the potential to do great harm; the latter can lead to better communication.

Adding salt to our speech is something to pray about. Clearly, we aren't doing anyone any good if we are trying to people-please with everything that comes out of our mouth. By the same token, too much salt will leave a bad taste in anybody's mouth. Therefore, let us pray for an appropriate amount of salt, as we speak the truth in love to others.

Holy Spirit, season my speech with your love. ⌐

Just for Today: I will add salt, as needed, to my conversations.

Angel in Training

Where you go, I will go;
where you lodge, I will lodge; . . .
Where you die, I will die—
there will I be buried.

—RUTH 1:16-17

After my best friend died, I felt completely lost and off balance in the early days of my grieving. Shortly after I went back to work, I remember wanting to wear a sign that read, "Friendless: Handle with Care." The world was proceeding with business as usual, while I remained frozen in grief, longing to turn back time.

As with any death or traumatic event, people tried their best to make me feel better. Some were very dear, while others weren't. A few compassionate souls seemed like angels in disguise. One of them was a man who had recently become a business associate. We were working on an impromptu assignment, and I felt I owed him an explanation for my general lack of concentration. After offering his heartfelt sympathy, he sternly proclaimed, "You need to go get yourself a massage."

This little bit of practical advice was just what I needed. I marveled at how he could have known that my body was screaming for comfort. The physical burden of grief can be excruciatingly hard on the body. The aches and pains seemed to come out of nowhere, and I felt like I was carrying the weight of the world.

I learned that the gentleman knew what I was going through, because as a Vietnam vet, he had lost more than one friend to suicide. It is a healing balm to connect with others who have experienced what we have experienced. Whether we call them kindred souls, guides, or guardian angels on earth, I am quite certain that when we are going through "the valley of the shadow of death," the Lord sends us special traveling companions—people who can walk a portion of the way beside us.

Then, when we finally reach the other side of the valley, we will have the awesome privilege of helping someone else. Because of our experience, we will be uniquely prepared to go where they go and lodge where they lodge, having already been there with an angel of our own.

Lord, thank you for the angels you've sent in my times of need. ⎯

Just for Today: I will ask the Lord how I can use my experiences to minister to others.

Life's Drama

The prayer of faith will save the sick,
and the Lord will raise them up.

—JAMES 5:15

Liz is a traveling nurse who works in operating rooms all over the country. From Alaska to the Virgin Islands, she has enjoyed practicing her profession in some of the most exciting and exotic places in the country. Yet, the awe and wonder of the part she plays in the healing of others remain fresh and new each time she enters the operating theater.

The term "operating theater" sounds rather poetic, and it reminds us that this is hallowed ground where the drama of life and death is played out every day. There is no other place where life hangs so closely in the balance. And according to Liz, it is a place where she and others experience the undeniable presence of God in a profoundly mysterious way.

Liz tells the story of a particular operation in which her assignment was to hold a man's heart in her hands while the doctors performed delicate surgery on his spine. With this awesome responsibility before her, Liz wrapped her fingers firmly around the heart. As she did, she noticed that its beat was somewhat erratic. Liz wondered whether the missing beats—which weren't significant enough to cause alarm—had registered on the monitor, or whether they were something that only she was able to detect.

She responded by bending closer into the open chest of the man and quietly praying that his heart would take on the rhythm of her own. After a short time, she noticed that it did. She could feel their two hearts beating as one. And for the next *six hours*, Liz stood over the man, her hands gently cupped around his heart. She couldn't move, rest, or take a break, because she was literally holding his life in her hands.

Most of us will never have the experience of holding someone's very life in our hands, but we *are* called to carry one another's burdens in the drama of life. We don't know when we will be asked to take on "supporting roles" as healers like Liz, but let us pray that our hearts will be ready when the curtain goes up!

Lord, you are awesome, and I praise your holy name. Use me to bring your life and healing to others. ⸺

Just for Today: I will seek out a heart-to-heart encounter with another.

Nothing but Joy

"*I have said these things to you so that my joy may be in you, and that your joy may be complete.*"

—JOHN 15:11

Joy is a wonderful gift. It isn't dependent upon circumstance or subject to any outside control or condition. No one can rob you of your joy without your permission. Joy isn't a feeling; it's a way of being. That's why the Letter of James told the early Christians that they should "consider it nothing but joy" whenever they faced trials (1:2). Enduring those trials would make them "mature and complete, lacking in nothing" (1:4).

We, too, can consider it "nothing but joy" that God sees fit to use us in his plan to love and serve others. It is truly awesome that the Creator of the universe would bestow on us talents and charisms to use in his name. He doesn't need us to accomplish anything, yet he wants each of us to be his partner, to participate in the deepest mystery of his joy. And it's possible for us to keep this joy, even when we face great tedium and trial.

Linda is a stay-at-home mother of five young children, who seems to radiate joy every time I see her.

Believe it or not, she doesn't appear to be superhuman, nor is she out of touch with reality! She has made the commitment to cultivate joy in her heart. She cooperates with God's grace to the best of her ability, even when she is almost at the end of her tether.

Linda is quick to say that she hasn't always been this way. Day by day, she is learning through her duties of making beds, wiping noses, folding laundry, and fixing dinner that in a very real way she is laying down her life for her husband and her children, and this brings her great joy.

The fact that she is fulfilling her vocation as a wife and mother and using the gifts God has given her brings her a confidence that is quiet and sure. She knows in her heart that God is actively involved in her life on a daily basis. He is giving her strength and infusing her with his joy to carry on in his name. This is the promise God makes to us when we lay down our lives: that our joy will be complete. And it just doesn't get any better than that!

Lord, fill me with joy, and show me the way that you would have me lay down my life for others. ⁓

Just for Today: I will reflect on the gifts and talents God has given me to serve others.

An Ever-Present Help

God is our refuge and strength,
a very present help in trouble.

—PSALM 46:1

Imagine that Jesus is standing behind you right now, with his hand planted on your shoulder. You feel a firm yet tender grip, a touch that tells you, "You belong to me." He is so near that you can feel his presence; it assures and encourages you. Imagine that you turn around and see Jesus looking down at you. He doesn't speak, but the tenderness of his eyes shows you that you are loved, accepted, treasured, and known. Your fears melt away, the tension in your body subsides, and you experience a deep sense of contentment and completion. As you reflect on this experience, you thank Jesus for his presence and care.

Jesus transformed the people of his day by his mere presence. His care and compassion inspired them to leave their families, friends, and possessions in order to follow him. The beautiful example of faith demonstrated by the woman with the hemorrhage, for example, shows that she was willing to go to great lengths just to touch his garment. His reputation as a teacher and healer was known throughout the land, and people sensed that he was truly different from all the others.

Jesus continues to care for the brokenhearted and hurting here on earth. Now, however, he invites us to stand in his place by showing his care and concern to those around us. Taking time to imagine how Jesus' caring presence surrounds us even now will help us to communicate it to others.

For so many, Jesus is merely an admirable historical figure. For others, his reputation has been buried under layers of misconceptions, fears, and disappointments. Some have been deeply betrayed and hurt by people acting in Jesus' name. Whether we have a troubled child, a depressed friend, a hurting husband, or someone else in our life who is in need, Jesus alone is our ever-present help, and he wants to use us as his instruments of caring in the world today.

Lord, reveal the depth of your caring heart, so that I might share it with others in need of your presence. ⟶

Just for Today: I will step aside from my daily routine and spend some time in reflection with Jesus.

God's Eyes

*"Blessed are your eyes, for they see, and your ears,
for they hear."*

MATTHEW 13:16

Roberta has been an inner-city social worker for more than twenty-five years. During her career, she has been spat on, shot at, lied to, and threatened. She has also been used as an instrument of God's profound love, acceptance, and peace. Quite amazingly, she remains enthusiastic and hopeful through it all. Even the most hardened heart or broken spirit is met with Roberta's unquenchable and upbeat spirit. When asked how she maintains her positive attitude, she said, "Every day I learn a little more about who God is through the people I meet. It's like going on an exciting adventure every time I go to work!" She calls these lessons "God moments," and they have sustained her through some of the toughest of times dealing with people and their brokenness.

Roberta's approach to her life's work is both humble and wise. She remains open and recognizes her own limitations in the face of sin, suffering, and pain. She allows herself to be used for God's purposes, to bring his light into some of the darkest places on earth. She leaves the results to him, and because of her willingness to hang in there, God has given her "new" eyes. She has been gifted with the ability to see his face in the faces of others, even those who don't appreciate or want her help. Far from becoming bitter or cynical, as others might, Roberta has used her daily encounters to enrich and deepen her relationship with God.

This type of grace-filled living is available to all of us as we serve our families and communities. We can remain hopeful in the face of great suffering and enthusiastic when we are faced with discouraging circumstances. We can choose, as Roberta has, to wait in joyful anticipation of the "God moments" that may lead us to deeper and more-meaningful discoveries about the love of God for others and ourselves.

Lord, give me eyes to see you in all the people with whom I come in contact today. ⌐

Just for Today: I will embrace my life as an adventure and look for the "God moments."

Perfect Love

Whoever fears has not reached perfection in love.

—1 JOHN 4:18

Fear is a formidable foe. It caused the disciples to chide Jesus when he stopped to talk with the woman at the well, and it caused Peter to deny Jesus after he had been arrested. Fear is what causes us to ignore, judge, compare, cast off, and condemn. Most of us don't even know the extent of the fear that keeps us from living as God intends.

For example, fear is what caused me to turn away from a woman who was beckoning me to cross the street as I was entering Mass one morning. I will never know what she wanted or needed. All I know is that she was obviously poor, distressed, and very *different* from me. So, I chose to pretend that she wasn't there.

As I was leaving Mass that day, I was suddenly struck with the image of Lazarus and the rich man. Remember the story? There was a grand banquet going on, attended by many friends of the rich man, as Lazarus lay hungry and sick at the gate. Lazarus was seen as nothing but an obstacle, an object to be kicked aside or ignored altogether. How convicted I was of my own sin and poverty when I thought of the banquet *I* had just participated in while this woman was left standing outside.

"There is no fear in love," the apostle John wrote, "but perfect love casts out fear" (1 John 4:18). So why are we so afraid to do the right thing, to take that first step toward healing, to love perfectly? It goes back to that first moment of fear, when Adam and Eve disobeyed God and hid themselves in shame. As a result, we live in an imperfect world where fear reigns.

Yet, there is hope that with God's grace, we will be able to overcome our fears and love more perfectly. The good news is that we serve a God of second chances; and just like the apostles, we will be presented with another opportunity, another Lazarus at the gate. Let us pray that this time we might have courage to invite him in.

Lord, cast out the fear in my heart that keeps me from loving others more perfectly. —

Just for Today: I will love without fear.

Let Go . . . Let God

Wisdom rescued from troubles those who served her.

—WISDOM 10:9

Our Lord has called us to serve one another. But is it possible to do too much for someone who is struggling? Believe it or not, it is—if we supply their needs so completely that we also take away their responsibility to help themselves. Whether they are our children, our friends, our spouse, or the rest of the world, people need the opportunity to learn from their mistakes. Failure is a necessary component of success. But if in helping others, we eliminate all risk that they might fail, we deprive them of an essential ingredient for growing into complete and whole human beings.

Unfortunately, many systems of care have created large populations of dependent people by robbing them of the dignity that comes from taking responsibility for their own circumstances. This can happen on a personal level, as well. An overprotective parent can blur the boundaries between healthy parental guidance that allows a child to grow and excessive control that leaves the child feeling helpless or smothered.

A well-meaning friend can sometimes become too involved when a crisis arises in the life of another. Sometimes a crisis is just what is needed to teach a valuable life lesson, and struggle is often a way to develop character. We don't want to interfere with God's plan for someone, in an overzealous attempt to be helpful.

If we encounter problems discerning the difference, a spiritual director or pastor can steer us clear of entanglements that might leave others feeling resentful of our efforts. A good indication that we might be crossing the line of compassion and overextending ourselves is when we experience heaviness, exhaustion, or confusion that won't go away.

It is perfectly okay to pull back when we encounter others who seem unable or unwilling to take proper responsibility for themselves. We can remain lovingly detached and clearly explain our own limits or the parameters of our helping. When we do, we will send a strong message of caring and concern by communicating our belief in their ability to help themselves.

Lord, help me to be wise when helping others and to detach with love when needed. ⌒

Just for Today: I will pray first before I act to ensure that I do not overstep my boundaries.

Daughters of Dignity

So God created humankind in his image,
in the image of God he created them;
male and female he created them.

—GENESIS 1:27

In his apostolic letter *Mulieris Dignitatem* (On the Dignity and Vocation of Women), Pope John Paul II quoted the words of his predecessor Pope Paul VI:

> "Within Christianity, more than in any other religion, and since its very beginning, women have had a special dignity. . . . It is evident that women are meant to form part of the living and working structure of Christianity in so prominent a manner that perhaps not all their potentialities have yet been made clear."[21]

Some interpret this statement to mean that women should seek equality with men in the priesthood. Others embrace it as a challenge to expand the role of women in the political or governmental structures of the Church. However, our former pope expressed something even more profound. He invited us, as Catholic women, to explore the depth and breadth of our spiritual influence and embrace the dignity that flows from our God-given vocations in the body of Christ.

Many of us have not been taught about our authentic feminine genius and the spiritual strength of its fruits. It is a strength we can neither measure materially nor achieve through our efforts alone. When we embrace the dignity of our true vocation, women become "an irreplaceable support and source of spiritual strength for other people, who perceive the great energies of [their] spirit. These 'perfect women' are owed much by their families, and sometimes by whole nations."[22]

When Jesus said to the Samaritan woman at the well, "If you knew the gift of God" (John 4:10), he was referring to himself and calling forth within her the gift she already possessed but was unaware of—her dignity. Jesus is saying the same to us as modern-day daughters of God. How can you more fully bring forth the gift of your feminine holiness and wholeness into the world to aid humanity today?

Lord, thank you for the gift of my femininity. Lead me toward a deeper understanding of this gift. ⟶

Just for Today: I will commit to reading Pope John Paul II's apostolic letter on the dignity of women.

Soul Friend

Wine and music gladden the heart,
but the love of friends is better than either.

—SIRACH 40:20

The Celtic culture includes a term for a special kind of friend known as an *anam cara,* or "soul friend." It's a beautiful form of friendship that recognizes the deep spiritual bond of communion between two souls. In his book titled *Anam Cara: A Book of Celtic Wisdom,* John O'Donohue described the *anam cara* as the person with whom "you could share your innermost self, your mind and your heart."[23]

This soul friendship is a bond of belonging that enables one to be completely authentic with another; it is a transforming friendship that brings spiritual clarity and an eternal understanding between two people. How many of us have a true soul friend with whom to share the deepest and most hidden parts of ourselves? Is your heart longing for just such a friend? If so, pray to Jesus to send you your anam cara.

Many women have sought godly friendships through prayer and met their soul friends as a result. Here's one example:

Carol was a new mother who was also reentering the Catholic Church. She began attending daily Mass with her infant daughter before going to work at her new job in a neighboring town. With virtually every area of her life bringing new experiences and challenges, Carol felt lost and lonely. She longed for a friend with whom to share her intimate thoughts about motherhood and the newfound joy of her faith.

Carol prayed for eight long months for the Lord to send her a friend. One day after daily Mass, a woman approached Carol and invited her to a monthly sharing meeting of women in town. Carol wholeheartedly agreed to attend. When she entered the room full of women, Carol was overwhelmed by the acceptance, love, and support she received. One woman in particular seemed to stand out from the rest. Carol felt an immediate kinship with her, and as it turned out, the woman felt the same instant connection. Their friendship blossomed as they discovered that they were indeed kindred souls, ordained by grace to share the journey of life together as true anam caras.

Lord, with you as my guide, show me how to be an anam cara. —

Just for Today: I will seek God's will for my friendships.

Love Always Wins

"But I say to you that listen, Love your enemies, do good to those who hate you, bless those who curse you, pray for those who abuse you."

—LUKE 6:27-28

If the cross of Christ teaches us anything, it is that love always wins. No matter what difficulties we encounter, what decisions we face, or what choices we make, when we choose love, we win. That is because love, by its very nature, is indestructible and unconquerable.

When Christ died on the cross, it looked as if love had been defeated. Even the apostles and other followers of Jesus were overcome with fear and despair and doubted his message.

Today we don't have to look very far to see the influence of evil in our world, and it's tempting to conclude that evil has won. On a personal level, we may be confronting the choice of whether to love or hate. Christ's message to us is to choose love, no matter what, and to accept his grace to carry out that decision.

There was a mother who was deeply anguished by her daughter's murder. This mother agonized and wrestled with the need to forgive the man who committed the crime. She felt imprisoned by her hatred and hardness of heart. For her, the decision to love was a complicated one. She wanted only to punish the man for the pain he had caused her daughter and her family. But in her heart, she knew that her desire for revenge would consume her and that her hatred would dishonor the memory of her beloved daughter.

So she chose love. She made a *decision* to forgive the man, regardless of her feelings, and vowed to pray for the murderer's soul on a daily basis. Each day, while barely able to utter his name, she included him in her prayers. Days turned to months and months into years, and something miraculous happened. The man confessed his sin and turned his life over to the Lord, while the woman's heart was softened and changed through her volunteer work ministering to prisoners. Love triumphed over sin and death through Jesus' resurrection, and love triumphs today every time we choose it over evil.

Lord, your cross is the proof that love conquers all. Help me to carry my own cross and choose love, even when it seems impossible to do. ⸺

Just for Today: I will choose love.

Tune-Up Time?

"For to all those who have, more will be given, and they will have an abundance; but from those who have nothing, even what they have will be taken away."

—MATTHEW 25:29

We are responsible for ensuring that our spiritual wells don't run dry. Being good stewards of our time and energy enables us to accomplish great things for the kingdom of God. Two parables in Matthew's gospel contain lessons about managing our time and resources: the parable of the ten bridesmaids and the parable of the talents. Both recommend a balanced approach: we shouldn't overextend ourselves to the point that we are emotionally and physically spent, but we shouldn't be so stingy with our investments that we conserve them to the point of making no meaningful investment at all.

God gives to each of us according to our own abilities. Some have more to give than others. The key is to know ourselves well enough to understand when we need to regroup and refuel our spiritual "engines." The best way to do this, of course, is through receiving Jesus in the Eucharist. Due to the demands on our personal resources, though, there may be times in our lives when daily Mass isn't possible. During those times, we can offer frequent spiritual communions.

Whenever a need presents itself, we have to decide how to respond on the basis of what we have to offer. Too often, we commit too quickly and do too much, running the risk of burning out or having to back out of commitments that we find we can't fulfill. Instead, we need to take time to assess our physical strength, financial resources, and time availability, and then turn to our heavenly Father to guide us and to provide where we might be lacking.

God can use us to the extent that we are ready, willing, and able. It's up to us to make sure we have the physical, spiritual, and emotional energy to walk in the footsteps of Jesus and meet the needs before us.

Lord, help me to be a good steward of all you've given me, so that I can use my gifts wisely. ⌐

Just for Today: I will take inventory of my emotional, physical, and spiritual reserves and make adjustments as needed.

Perfect Sacrifice

The sacrifice acceptable to God is a broken spirit;
a broken and contrite heart, O God, you will not despise.

—PSALM 51:17

Here's a thought: doing all the right things is no guarantee that all the things will turn out right. But sometimes we get caught up in that kind of thinking, don't we? Then we get very discouraged, maybe even disgruntled, when things don't turn out the way we think they should. The older brother in the story of the prodigal son was someone who did all the right things. He didn't disrespect his father by squandering his inheritance, and he didn't leave home (which, in those days, was quite an insult to the father). He worked and assumed responsibility, while his brother ran off to play hooky for all those years. The elder son was a good fellow, to be sure.

Yet, who ended up getting all the goodies? It seems like the younger brother should have received a punishment, not a party. Being perfect didn't pay off for the older brother like he thought it would. He was doing all the right things, but as we learn in the course of the story, he was doing them for the wrong reasons!

He thought that his faithfulness would earn him his inheritance. An important lesson of the story of the prodigal son is that our motives count.

The Lord can see what remains hidden in the depth of our hearts. He knows when we are seeking to "earn our way" into heaven through our good deeds. He knows when we covet our perfect scores more than the purity of our actions. He also understands our human nature and has given us the Holy Spirit to reveal our motives to us. We don't need to be overly concerned with analyzing our every action, but it's good to have a gentle awareness of our inner tendencies toward hidden pride and perfectionism.

A contrite heart is a heart that's willing to admit its mistakes and hidden motives. A broken spirit is one that simply accepts its imperfections with grace and gratitude for a God who alone is perfect. We can offer our imperfections to God with confidence, knowing that we are acceptable to him just the way we are.

Thank you, Lord, for the light of the Holy Spirit and your merciful judgments of my actions. ⌒

Just for Today: I will examine my motives in a particular relationship or area of my life, asking the Holy Spirit to illuminate my heart and mind.

The Opposite of Love

"Lord, when was it that we saw you . . .
sick or in prison, and did not take care of you?"
—MATTHEW 25:44

The opposite of love isn't hate; it's indifference. I experienced this reality one morning at a convenience store. Approaching the door to go in, I was met with a startling sight. A man, hunched over, held on to the door for what literally looked like his life. He was emaciated, drooling, filthy, and obviously under the influence of drugs.

This man was close to death, and yet people were going about their business as usual—as if he wasn't even there. As disturbing as the scene was, I admit that I, too, went into the store without acknowledging him. I was hoping he would be gone when I left the store, for I knew that it was going to be impossible for me to walk by him a second time.

Sure enough, he was stooped against the building as I exited. I knelt down, asking how I could help. To my surprise, the man met my gaze. In his eyes, I saw something that bordered on preposterous, given his circumstances. I saw a glimmer of hope.

At that moment, it struck me with great clarity that either we choose to love or we just don't care. So, I pleaded with the manager to call an ambulance instead of the police. I sat with the man, stroked his hand, and tried to get him to drink some water. I did what I could, but I am still haunted by thoughts that I didn't do enough. Such is the burden of love.

As the ambulance pulled away, I wept, not from sadness, but from awe that God would allow me the honor of meeting him in the disguise of a "hopeless" drug addict—a man named Anthony, who told me that I reminded him of his sister. I will never forget my last glimpse of him as he raised his dirt-encrusted hand to bless me with the sign of the cross. His faint but undeniable smile still burns in my memory and warms my heart. Such is the reward of love.

Lord, thank you for the opportunity to love you and serve you in your most distressing disguise. Open my eyes to recognize you. ——

Just for Today: I will pray for freedom for Anthony and for all who are in bondage to addiction.

Good Fruit

"And seeing a fig tree by the side of the road, he went to it and found nothing at all. . . . Then he said to it, 'May no fruit ever come from you again!'"

—MATTHEW 21:19

The older we get, the more experienced we become in discriminating between what is necessary in our lives and what is not. Our tastes grow more refined, and we become more selective about how we spend our time, and with whom. We are more likely to conserve our energy and efforts, and as a result, we can get a little "set in our ways."

Given this tendency, we have to take care to not become closed minded or grow rigid in our expectations and interactions with others. When Jesus cursed the fig tree in Matthew 21:19, he was railing against a condition that can also affect the human heart. If we aren't careful, our heart can dry up and grow hardened and unproductive. As we age, we don't want to outlive our usefulness and cease to bear good fruit. We can keep that from happening as long as we continue to allow Jesus to plant his seeds of mercy, love, and compassion within us.

Just as the seasons in nature render different "fruits" of our labor, so do the seasons in our lives. What we call the golden years can either be a time of great productivity and a rich culmination of all we have learned and experienced, or they can be a time of decline and decay. To the extent that we remain open to God's generous provision within our hearts, we will continue to bear good and useful fruit.

We always have the potential to offer ourselves or to contribute something of value to others. God wants to till the soil of our hearts for his great harvest, right up to our last breath. Let us remain open to his abundance, so that we can continue to offer a generous yield to others.

Heavenly Father, fill me to overflowing with the fruit of your love, and let my life be an expression of your great abundance. ⌒

Just for Today: I will choose one of the fruits of the Holy Spirit as they are presented by the Church— charity, joy, peace, patience, kindness, goodness, generosity, gentleness, faithfulness, modesty, self- control, or chastity—to reflect upon, learn about, and express more fully throughout the day.

Go Gently

Let your adornment be the inner self with the lasting beauty
of a gentle and quiet spirit, which is very precious
in God's sight.

—1 PETER 3:4

It seems as if the mantra of our modern times is much like the motto of a recent Olympics—"faster, higher, stronger." While these values may be good for a worldwide sporting competition, they cannot sustain us in our daily lives, and they are in conflict with the life of our spirits. Our souls are longing to embrace another way.

Rather than "faster, higher, stronger," might we instead go "slowly, deeply, gently" into life? Slowly, deeply, gently. . . . A lack of gentleness can lead to a lack of mercy or concern for others—such as when we get caught up in competition at all cost. And when we lose our ability to be truly connected with others, we lose our ability to be connected to ourselves.

Two apostles, James and John, fell into this trap. They were seeking a primary place in the kingdom of God, letting their ambitions get the better of them. They were neither quiet nor gentle in their spirits. Contrast their behavior with the meekness and quietude of Jesus.

In Isaiah 42:1-4, Jesus is described by God as

> my servant, whom I uphold,
>   my chosen, in whom my soul delights;
> I have put my spirit upon him;
>   he will bring forth justice to the nations.
> He will not cry or lift up his voice,
>   or make it heard in the street;
> a bruised reed he will not break,
>   and a dimly burning wick he will not quench.

With Mary as our model, let us live out the words of Ben Sirach in Sirach 3:17-18: "My child, perform your tasks with humility; / then you will be loved by those whom God accepts. / The greater you are, the more you must humble yourself; / so you will find favor in the sight of the Lord."

Slowly, deeply, gently . . . yes.

Dear Lord, help me to embrace a life of gentleness and connection with others. Give me the grace to let go of the need to compete, and let my life be an outpouring of tender love and mercy. ⸺

Just for Today: I will offer a gentle expression of concern to someone.

Into the Deep

> *"Put out into the deep water and let down
> your nets for a catch."*
>
> —LUKE 5:4

Now more than at any other time in history, we are at risk of drowning in superficiality. We can access an almost infinite amount of information at the touch of a button, yet we are slipping further and further away from the truth. We have more possessions than we ever thought possible and have much less substance. We have technology that lets us converse with someone on the other side of the globe whom we will never meet, while we are losing the capacity to be genuine, authentic, and intimate with others right here at home. The rich dimensions of the human heart are being obscured as we expand our range but lose our depth.

When Jesus appeared after his resurrection to Peter, he initiated a profound encounter with his friend. Three times, Jesus asked, "Simon son of John, do you love me?" (John 21:15-17). By asking this question, not once, but three times, Jesus was inviting Peter to go deeper and deeper into his way of love, mercy, and forgiveness. For each one of us, that invitation still stands today.

Etty Hillesum was a deep thinker and writer who died in Auschwitz at the age of twenty-nine. Though she was Jewish, her spiritual journey led her to read the New Testament and the lives of the saints with great passion. Her writings are contained in the book *Etty Hillesum: An Interrupted Life and Letters from Westerbork* and reflect a profound understanding of the mystery of the cross in the years she was confined in occupied Amsterdam, before being transferred to the death camps.

Hillesum wrote, "There is a really deep well inside me. And in it dwells God. Sometimes I am there too. But more often stones and grit block the well, and God is buried beneath. Then God must be dug out again."[24]

What are the stones and grit that are in God's way in your heart? How will you respond to the Lord's invitation to enter more deeply into his love? Truly, God draws us with his questions and guides us along a path to a deeper place of knowing. Let us answer him with our willingness to go beneath the surface to find him.

Lord, give me ears to hear the questions you pose to my innermost being. —

Just for Today: I will listen deeply.

Opportunity of Suffering

For it is better to suffer for doing good,
if suffering should be God's will,
than to suffer for doing evil.

—1 PETER 3:17

The problem of suffering confronts us all; we will not escape it. If by chance you have not experienced significant suffering yet, then you have probably witnessed someone else's suffering. It's as integral to life as taking a breath, and we cannot live fully unless we are willing to suffer. Trying to avoid suffering is one of life's cruelest paradoxes, for to do so only increases our pain.

While suffering may remain life's greatest mystery, we can still find meaning in it. At the canonization of St. Teresa Benedicta of the Cross, Pope John Paul II said that "the true message of suffering is a lesson of love. Love makes suffering fruitful and suffering deepens love."[25] In Romans 5:3-4, St. Paul wrote that "suffering produces endurance, and endurance produces character, and character produces hope."

Injustice, profound loss, and every kind of emotional and physical suffering present us with a sacred opportunity for personal transformation and a means to a deeper, more richly lived life. Suffering may lead to a confrontation with long-lost hurts, to the embrace of dreams we were once afraid to pursue, or to greater authenticity and integrity in our lives. Suffering speaks a new language of the heart and offers a different way of seeing and relating to God through every moment of our suffering and beyond.

Ultimately, our suffering has the potential to grace us with a Godlike compassion that enables us to walk with others as they suffer. Mother Teresa said, "The suffering ones are the closest to God; they receive his kiss."[26]

God neither demands nor dismisses our suffering. Completely compassionate, he enters into our suffering with us and redeems it for our sake and the sake of others. We serve a God who was and is willing to suffer for the salvation of our souls. When the season of suffering is upon us, may we be convinced that God does not allow us to suffer the dark storms of life without also giving us the opportunity to see or be a greater light as a result.

Lord, give me the courage to look for meaning in the suffering around me. ⟶

Just for Today: I will bring comfort to a suffering soul.

Doing Too Much

Whatever you do, do everything for the glory of God.

—1 CORINTHIANS 10:31

Presenting a talk for Christian women who were struggling with the "superwoman syndrome" of trying to be all things to all people all the time (sound familiar?), I asked them to reflect on how they know when they are doing too much. One woman replied, "I know I'm doing too much when the approval of others becomes more important than the approval of God."

With incredible insight, this woman had not only defined the symptom but articulated the essence of the problem! Trying to please people instead of God can become a real trap for us. Nurturing relationships and seeking harmony are among our God-given attributes, and so we can easily sense the displeasure or disapproval of others. As a result, we can become overly sensitive to the opinions of others and overcompensate by doing too much to make them happy.

We want people to see that we are good and giving. We want them to be happy and agree with us. For the most part, life is nicer when we meet with the approval of others, and there's nothing wrong with that. But when we go down that slippery slope of seeking human recognition and acceptance before we seek God, then we may be doing too much of a good thing.

The woman who answered the question reflected further and concluded, "I feel less free in my spirit when I am always trying to please people. It's my way of trying to control their reactions and opinions of me. On the other hand, when I am trying to please God, it feels better, because I know I am striving to do his will, and that's always the right thing to do."

God's will is not for us to win the approval of those around us. Doing the best we can in any given situation is *always* enough. Remembering that there's absolutely nothing we can do that God can't do better will help us to keep our focus where it needs to be—on him.

Lord, you know my good intentions and my heart. Guide me in my desire to seek you first, above all things, and to put into perspective the opinions of others. ⌐

Just for Today: I will seek God's approval first.

Never Too Late

*But Jesus answered them, "My Father is still working,
and I also am working."*

—JOHN 5:17

God wants you to know that it is never too late for him to change you or someone else. It is never too late to learn more about him, to live more fully, or to love more freely. If you have dreams yet to be fulfilled, take heart, because God is still at work in your life. There is still time for you to answer his call to a particular vocation or embrace a new direction in your life.

If you have deep regrets or wounds, or if you are praying for someone who does, remember that there is no statute of limitations on God's forgiveness. Recovery and healing are always possible. There is still time to be transformed and converted, because in God's eyes, there are no hopeless causes. No person or situation is too far gone; no soul is beyond rescue. St. Paul spoke to this in his letter to the Ephesians, when he wrote, "But God, who is rich in mercy, out of the great love with which he loved us even when we were dead, . . . made us alive together with Christ" (2:4-5).

In fact, throughout the Bible, we are introduced to people who were saved from situations that seemed hopeless, such as Jairus's daughter, who was thought to be dead, and the self-mutilating demoniac who incoherently wandered the countryside. The man who sat by the healing pool for twenty-eight years and the woman with the issue of blood suffered many years before they were healed. Whether dead in spirit or dead in their physical bodies, God's love had the power to heal and transform them.

An ancient Roman saying proclaims, "As long as there is breath, there is hope." Truly, God's hand is upon us, even when we don't know it. He is always at work, going to battle against the devil's greatest tool—discouragement. When left unchecked, discouragement can grow from sarcasm, cynicism, and self-sufficiency into hopelessness, despair, and spiritual death. Discouragement tricks us into thinking that God's lifeboat has left our harbor, never to return. Don't believe it! It is never too late to receive new life in Christ.

Lord, help me to persevere in trust, as you work in my life and the lives of those I pray for. ⎯

Just for Today: I will believe that change is possible.

Having the Last Word

The word of God is living and active, sharper than any two-edged sword.

—Hebrews 4:12

A national study has revealed that we are exposed to almost sixteen thousand bits of information each day. This includes messages we receive from other people, the computer, television, and radio and from what we read, study, or even pass by on the way to work. We can't control many of these images, and they contribute to a modern-day condition called "information overload." In fact, the study reported that we learn more in a day than those who lived in Jesus' time learned in an entire lifetime!

The consequences of instant information and non-stop communication have yet to be seen. However, today's parents have a pretty good sense of the difficulties this phenomenon is creating in their children's lives. One mother explained that she feels like she is "battling a daily tidal wave" as she attempts to control the influx of information that is forming her children's character without their even realizing it. In response, we cannot lock our children away in remote ivory towers, as tempting as that might be. Instead, we are challenged to come up with creative ways to get their attention and to help them ultimately discern for themselves what information they will take in and what they will leave behind.

One thing that we can be sure of is that when we expose our children to the truth that we know through our faith and God's word, our children will be "armed" with a double-edged sword that cuts through the harmful effects of the untruth and confusion that surrounds them. One of the greatest skills our children can learn is how to use the Bible as a resource guide for life. We can get them started when they are very young by teaching them one verse at a time. The timeless truths of Scripture will sustain them and help them sort through the onslaught of information headed their way.

Lord, help me to teach my children well and to show them the value of your word for all seasons. ⟶

Just for Today: I will help my children memorize a Scripture verse that applies to their life situation.

A Mother Is a Teacher

She opens her mouth with wisdom,
and the teaching of kindness is on her tongue.

—PROVERBS 31:26

Henry Ward Beecher once said, "The mother's heart is the child's schoolroom."[27] It can be daunting to realize that as we become mothers, we also become teachers, whether we choose to or not. Our children are watching and learning from us with every passing day. From the moment of our first embrace, they begin observing and absorbing information about themselves, their world, and some of the most important aspects of life.

Clearly, we will never have all the answers, and we cannot completely understand every situation and challenge our children will face. Just as there are no perfect parents, there are no perfect teachers, either. We can only strive to be present to our children, to be approachable and authentic. It's okay to tell them that we don't know something, because in doing so, we teach them humility. It's okay to reveal a personal fault, because by attempting to overcome it, we teach them integrity and strength of character. More than anything else, our children need us to be genuinely human.

St. Francis de Sales said, "Do not wish to be anything but what you are, and try to be that perfectly." He was the same saint who said, "Be patient with all things, but first of all with yourself." Both bits of wisdom serve us well in our dual vocation as mother and teacher. They remind us to treat ourselves with the same respect and gentle acceptance we extend to our children when we encourage them to do their best without agonizing over their imperfections.

No doubt, we learned from our own mothers that "actions speak louder than words." Our children will always learn more from what we do (or don't do) than from what we say. Reflect on the unspoken lessons you've learned from your mother, and think about the lessons your own children have learned or may be learning from you. Then ask the Holy Spirit, the teacher of your soul, to guide you, knowing that his lesson plan is the best one of all!

Lord, fill me with your grace, and give my children (and me) a teachable and reachable spirit. ——

Just for Today: I will make a list of my life's greatest lessons.

A Healthy Fear

The fear of the Lord is the crown of wisdom.

—SIRACH 1:18

The phrase "fear of the Lord" appears in the Scriptures more than a hundred times. For many, it's a confusing concept. Does it mean that we should be afraid of God? Is it the kind of fear that creates anxiety and shame as we relate to him as a disapproving father? Some of us have struggled to accept God's love because of a strained or dysfunctional relationship with our earthly fathers. The command to fear the Lord only seems to complicate the matter further.

The Scriptures also say, "There is no fear in love" (1 John 4:18). How is it that we are commanded to love and fear God at the same time? The answers to these questions are made clearer in the Book of Sirach, which says, "Those who fear the Lord seek to please him. . . . Those who fear the Lord prepare their hearts" (2:16-17). These clarifications help to broaden the definition of fear and deepen our understanding of our two-way relationship with God.

A proper fear of God is an acknowledgment of our limitations and his limitlessness. We accept our incompleteness and his omnipotence. We embrace our poverty and his provision. We recognize our place and give reverence to his. Then our hearts are prepared to receive the awesome gift of wisdom that flows from our right relationship with him. Growing in wisdom doesn't mean that we will have all the answers, but it teaches us to embrace all our questions. Wisdom enables us to remain docile and rest gently in the arms of God's mystery.

Quite simply, fear of the Lord helps us to resist putting God "in a box." It is holy and healthy and puts all of our lesser fears to rest. These lesser fears lead to idolatry and are the by-product of our attempts to control what we don't know and can't understand. Scriptural fear of the Lord will always lead to greater freedom and wholeness. It expands our spirits and fills our souls with awe and reverence for our God, who is not only wise but infinitely loving and patient, as well.

Lord, help me to grow in wisdom and understanding of who you are. ⁓

Just for Today: I will quietly rest in the mystery of God.

Love's Chance

Each of you must give as you have made up your mind.
—2 CORINTHIANS 9:7

For many years, my family and I frequented a diner called the "Last Chance" for Friday-night fish dinners. Each week, we joined the other regular customers—an assortment of truck drivers, young families, bikers, and others. Our waitress always greeted us with open arms and a full coffee pot. On one particular night, however, the usually light and friendly atmosphere seemed different.

We soon found out why. John—who co-owned the restaurant with his young wife, Lisa—was in the final stages of a fast-acting form of brain cancer. He wasn't going to make it. As soon as she saw us, Lisa trudged to our table, pulled up a chair, and collapsed in exhaustion and grief. She began to tell her story in a flurry of words and sobs. She had only dared to leave her husband's side for the dinner-hour rush, just to get a break from her round-the-clock care in what was sure to be his last days.

We listened intently as Lisa poured her heart out, barely noticing the lone waitress buzzing around, tending to the customers who were streaming into the restaurant. As time went on and the place filled up, I noticed that every now and then, customers would get up and help themselves to a cup of coffee and offer it to those seated at the next table. Later I noticed one of the regulars behind the counter making salads and passing out bread.

Suddenly, Lisa jumped up and scrambled to the kitchen, explaining that she was the only cook on duty that night. It dawned on us that the entire clientele of the restaurant had been waiting patiently for service and for Lisa to finish sharing her pain with us at the table. Unbelievably, she had talked for almost half an hour! During that time, no one complained or walked out. Every patron seemed to understand, and some even took it upon themselves to fill in the gaps quietly and unobtrusively until Lisa was ready to return to her duties.

Great love is found in the little things we do for others, and it surely was the "special" on the menu that night.

Lord, help me to love quietly and generously today.

Just for Today: I will make myself available to hear someone else's story.

A Mother's Faith

*Now faith is the assurance of things hoped for,
the conviction of things not seen.*

—HEBREWS 11:1

When a mother watches her little child get on the school bus and head off to kindergarten for the first time, her heart may be filled with a swirling eddy of emotions—pride, loss, sadness, nostalgia, excitement, joy, and fear—all with a little faith mixed in. As these feelings converge on her, faith alone keeps her from running after the school bus to overtake it and pull her child back into the safety of her arms. She cannot see what the day will bring for her little one, but her faith assures her that God will be watching, too, and that all of her hopes and dreams for her child will be waiting on the other side of that closed school bus door.

Over and over again, through the course of her child's life, a mother's faith will be tested. The first jump into the deep end quickly becomes the first day of college, and through it all we are faced with the choice to either live by faith or live in fear of all that we cannot know for sure. One mother's play on words captures the essence of faith; instead of referring to the "true gift of faith," she calls it "the true grit of faith." I think she may have a point!

Faith means that we believe, in spite of the physical evidence and knowledge we gather through our own five senses. Faith sometimes seems to go against reason. Some people confuse faith for mere intuition, personal perception, or strong human desire. Faith is neither manipulation nor magical thinking. It is a commitment we make in the way we approach all the unknowns and first steps in our lives. Faith means that we live our lives with our arms and hearts wide open. Faith is truly a hidden treasure in a mother's heart, a free gift from God that we open day by day, as we trust in his goodness with all our might.

Dear Lord, help me to persevere in my faith, even when I am afraid or faltering. Teach me to stay open and eager to receive the gift of faith every day of my life. —

Just for Today: I will open the gift of faith.

Running the Race

Let us run with perseverance the race that is set before us.
—HEBREWS 12:1

Kathy, an accomplished track-and-field athlete who excelled in all the events, was asked which was her favorite. She replied that the hurdles were what she enjoyed the most. Instead of selecting a sport that required a shorter distance or a cleaner path, she favored the hurdles, because they required not only speed but agility and endurance, as well. When asked why she didn't pursue an easier sport, Kathy replied that she liked a challenge, and that the tougher the challenge, the greater the reward at the finish line.

When it comes to life, we all face a similar choice of which course to take. We can either follow the easier path or the more difficult one. When we choose, as Kathy did, to take the road less traveled, we do so with faith that it will bring us the greater reward. In spiritual terms, we call this taking up our cross and following Christ or going through the narrow gate.

In fact, our spiritual walk is a lot like a hurdle race, in that it demands endurance and sure-footedness as we negotiate obstacles along the way. Just as hurdles are an integral part of the race, so will each obstacle play a necessary part in our progress toward the finish line of heaven. Far from perceiving the hurdles as barriers, Kathy explains that they are what push her to move forward during the race. The requirement to jump and scale the hurdle is a helpful boost, and not a hopeless hindrance, to her progress.

Likewise, we can view life's hurdles not as barriers to bring us down, but as the very events, circumstances, and challenges that will move us closer to our goal. With God's grace, we can, like Kathy and St. Paul, rise to the challenge and persevere to the end, despite the obstacles that stand in our way.

Lord, help me to remember that every hurdle can help me when I offer it up to you. ⸺

Just for Today: I will thank God for the hurdles in my life and look for ways in which they can help me grow.

Serenity Under Stress

*"O God, whose might is over all, hear the voice
of the despairing. . . .
And save me from my fear!"*

—ESTHER C 14:19

Nancy was experiencing stress in virtually every area of her life. Her husband had a debilitating heart condition, while her daughter was coping with a difficult divorce. Nancy's job was in jeopardy, and her closest friend was moving three states away. Any one of these factors would have been enough to cause tremendous anxiety, but the combination of all of them at once was almost unbearable.

In the midst of the crises, Nancy poured her heart out to a friend, saying, "I'm trying to stay strong for everyone else, but I just can't cope anymore!" Her friend suggested that instead of struggling to be strong and stoic in the storm, she might strive to model self-care, compassion, and respect for her own needs and limitations. Her friend also intimated that good coping doesn't necessarily mean being in control all the time. Rather, she said, coping is actually more about letting go.

When stress threatens our well-being, we have a choice to make: we can ignore it, we can fight it, or we can respect it.

Many of us choose the first option, but we soon learn that ignoring our stress doesn't make it go away. It just forces it underground, where it can manifest in another way, usually as a physical ailment. This reaction to stress can cause a great deal of internal physical and emotional damage without our even realizing it.

If we fight our stress, we run the risk of not only hurting ourselves but hurting others, as well. The battle will spill into our relationships, and there will be no satisfactory resolution. Far from alleviating it, this reaction to stress usually creates more of it.

When we respect stress, we have the best chance of reducing its negative effects. Our strength comes when we step back and listen to our own heart's and body's reaction to stress. Self-care could mean anything from taking a bath to taking an extended vacation, but it will be something that nurtures and nourishes us—a true act of self-respect.

Lord, when I am overwrought with anxiety, teach me how to take care of myself, let go, and rest in you. —

Just for Today: I will perform a loving act of self-care.

The Gift of Compassion

If then there is any encouragement in Christ, . . .
any compassion and sympathy . . . be of the same mind,
having the same love.

—Philippians 2:1-2

Most of us recognize the limitations of others and accept them. We don't dwell on their weaknesses, and we are usually compassionate and understanding when they are struggling with some personal problem or challenge. As mothers we are especially sensitive to our children, and far from condemning them when they make mistakes, we offer encouragement and even relish the teaching moment. We understand that their mistakes are a necessary part of their growth and feel only a sense of tenderness as we help to mend their broken pride.

If we can extend this loving acceptance to others, then why are we so hard on ourselves? Are we willing to embrace our own shortcomings and brokenness with a spirit of gentleness and compassion?

Compassion means "to suffer with," and it is as important to be able to put up with our own faults as it is to be compassionate with others. St. Thérèse of Lisieux keenly understood this concept and advised her sister in a letter, "If you are willing to bear serenely the trial of being displeasing to yourself, then you will be . . . [for Jesus] a pleasant place of shelter"[28]

When we are willing to suffer with our imperfect selves, we are offering a humble heart to Jesus and creating a place where he can reveal his love and mercy freely and authentically. "Perfect" people have no need for Jesus; there is no room for him in their hearts. Indeed, it is most often through our failures and brokenness, not our successes, that God can draw nearer to us, and we, to him.

We can trust him enough to share our mistakes and shortcomings, our struggles and shame. The tenderness that we offer to others is a gift we can give to ourselves. We serve a compassionate God. When we stumble and fall, he is there to help us up again.

We have the choice to treat ourselves with compassion or condemnation. Which one will you choose?

Lord, I pray to receive the gift of your compassion and mercy so that I can offer it to others and to myself.

Just for Today: I will be mindful of the ways in which I am harsh and self-critical and give myself the gift of compassion.

Wisdom Passed On

The beginning of wisdom is the most sincere desire
for instruction.

—WISDOM 6:17

Mary's visit to Elizabeth shortly after the annunciation is usually understood as a mission to assist her elder relative in preparation for the birth of John the Baptist. A more likely scenario, however, is that the visit afforded Elizabeth the opportunity to pass down wisdom to her younger kinswoman, a tradition of sharing that has gone on throughout human history.

In a special way, women are usually the memory keepers in the family. They collect photographs, keep scrapbooks, and record family history. Women readily share their memories and stories of the heart, passing down family lore and wisdom from one generation to the next. Our mothers, grandmothers, and great-grandmothers have a wealth of knowledge and mother wit to share with us about how to raise our daughters and sons and how to influence our world today and for the future.

The Scriptures reflect the value of having elders in our midst. The book of Sirach says, "How attractive is sound judgment in the gray-haired, and for the aged to possess good counsel! How attractive is wisdom in the aged. . . . Rich experience is the crown of the aged, and their boast is the fear of the Lord" (25:4-6).

We owe so much to the women (and men) who have gone before us. They have seen more changes in the world than any generation before them. If you haven't already, seek out your elders—whether they are a part of your family, your church, or your community—and ask them to share with you from the rich well of their life experiences. Perhaps you could initiate a Wisdom Circle in your parish or neighborhood senior center, where seniors could tell their stories and share the lessons they have learned in their lives with younger generations. Their wisdom will enrich you, and you will be the better for it—and so will your children and your children's children.

Lord, I cherish your wisdom. Lead me to the teachers I need here on earth, so that I might learn from their experience and grow wise in my own time. ⌐

Just for Today: I will seek out an elder and listen to his or her story.

What If . . .

"What is born of the Spirit is spirit. . . . The wind blows
where it chooses, . . . but you do not know where it comes
from or where it goes. So it is with everyone
who is born of the Spirit."

—JOHN 3:6, 8

Art Linkletter used to say that "kids say the darnedest things." Children also ask some of the most profound questions! They seem to have an inner clarity of spirit that we adults lost long ago. Sammy, age eight, wondered, "What if everybody in the whole world laughed at the same time? What would it sound like?" Good question! Sammy wasn't trying to be a junior philosopher; he just thought it might be neat if it could happen.

"What if" questions are packed with powerful potential and can lead us on a wonderful adventure in imagination and possibility. When we lose touch with our spiritual capacity to wonder, or when our lives become all about a quest for having every answer, we miss something special and important about our journey here. "What if . . ." opens new doors of opportunity and frees us to explore beyond what we think we know. In fact, it may have been God's own "what if" question that sparked the creation of the universe and every soul that he's created since!

As adults, we get caught up in the practical "what ifs," such as, What if I don't go to that family reunion? or What if my boss finds out that I didn't do that report? We rarely ask these questions about a mystery: the consequences are usually understood. Our questions are more of a combination of wishful thinking and resignation than a whimsical quest for the unknown. But it doesn't have to be that way. Somewhere within us, there is still a child fascinated by life's mysteries.

"What if" adventures have created vaccines to cure millions and put human beings on the moon. They have inspired movements of change (for better and worse) and have been the first step toward making life-long dreams come true. We all have the Spirit of God within us, which means that we all have the capacity to wonder. Do you have a personal "what if" question? What hopes, dreams, and mental meanderings do you wish to pursue? What if you could?

Oh Lord, send your Holy Spirit to inspire me, and restore my sense of wonder. —

Just for Today: I will embark on a "what if" adventure.

Purpose and Joy

*For it is God who is at work in you,
enabling you both to will and to work for his
good pleasure.*

—PHILIPPIANS 2:13

There's a beautiful dance that takes place between two intertwined treasures of the heart: purpose and joy. Our greatest joy comes when we express ourselves through the unfolding of our purpose. And our purpose most often flows from living our life "poised for joy."

Many people spend a good part of their lives searching for a purpose as if it were something far outside the boundaries of their present circumstance. This quest for meaning can carry us away from the very purpose for which we were created. Cardinal John Henry Newman expressed his certainty of our God-given purpose in a beautiful prayer: "God has created me to do him some definite service. He has committed to me some work which he has not committed to another. I have a mission. . . . He has not created me for naught."[29]

The truth is that if we are living our lives faithfully and trusting that God is at work in our day-to-day lives, we are free to experience the joy and blessings that come when we embrace our current circumstance, no matter what it may be. If you are a wife and mother, then rest assured that you are fulfilling your purpose. If you are single and involved in the world of work, you are fulfilling your purpose. If you are a retired widow, you are fulfilling your purpose.

That doesn't mean that we won't still have yearnings and dreams to fulfill; we may still have some inner rumblings that urge us to seek a greater significance. We can take these inner longings to prayer and ask the Lord to guide our steps. When we are poised for joy—ready to experience joy in whatever form it takes—and willing to use the talents God has given us in his service, we can be confident that he will lead us to whatever purpose he has for us. Cardinal Newman's prayer goes on to say, "I will trust Him, whatever, wherever I am. I can never be thrown away." In other words, it is never too late to uncover the treasure of purpose and joy that God has for us here and in his kingdom to come.

Heavenly Father, I am grateful for my life and its purpose. May I receive your joy through the "work" of my soul and my life. ——

Just for Today: I will be poised for joy.

In God's Hands

We know that all things work together for good for those who love God.

—ROMANS 8:28

Martha had been praying for more than three years that her two adult daughters would mend a rift between them that was tearing apart their entire family. In an attempt to bring the two together, she tried everything from writing pleading letters to holding expensive family reunions, but nothing she did worked. In fact, her efforts just seemed to make matters worse. It broke her heart to watch division and strife poison her family, as the other siblings lined up to "take sides" in the dispute.

Martha finally threw up her hands in prayer (not despair) and submission and gave the whole situation to God. Some might say that she gave up; others might say she gave in; but handing any situation over to God is neither of these. Resignation and surrender are not the same. One resigns with regret, but one surrenders with confidence.

The truth is that when Martha stepped out of the middle of the situation between her daughters, God had room to step in. Shortly before Advent, she received a phone call from one of the daughters. The young woman was coming home for Christmas for the first time in three years. The other daughter involved in the dispute lived in the same town as Martha. Could this be an answer to her prayers?

It took a tremendous amount of grace and spiritual discipline for Martha to sit back and let the holidays unfold. She trusted the Lord, all right, but she wasn't too sure of her family's ability to come together peacefully. Still, she placed her hope in God's hands, and throughout the holidays, she witnessed a beautiful spiritual and emotional healing taking place between her daughters. Eventually her entire family was restored.

Martha was finally able to celebrate the gift of her family, as she rejoiced in God's faithfulness. Reflecting on the experience, she remarked, "God was all over it!" It was one more opportunity for her to embrace Romans 8:28 and claim it for her own.

Lord, I praise you for your faithfulness and grace, which enable me to surrender my life into your hands.——

Just for Today: I will hand over a problem or trial to the Lord, expecting good to come from it.

To Be Perfect or Not to Be

"Be perfect, therefore, as your heavenly Father is perfect."
—MATTHEW 5:48

A particular writing exercise requires you to leave a known mistake or imperfection in a manuscript for a week before making any attempt to correct it. Every day, you must read your manuscript, keeping track of your inner tolerance for the error. It drives most people crazy to keep the flaw in until the end of the week. But that's the whole point!

The purpose of the exercise is to confront perfectionism and that old, familiar, critical inner voice. It teaches the writer to be comfortable with what is, instead of what should be. The lesson of accepting our mistakes helps us put them in perspective and brings them into balance with our accomplishments. It sounds like a good exercise for life, doesn't it?

In fact, ancient Greek artisans purposefully left imperfections in their creations so as not to be considered arrogant by the gods. For them, imperfection wasn't only acceptable, it was expected, and it was an assurance that they weren't in competition with the deities. Although the ancient Greeks' methods may seem primitive to us, there is some wisdom to their ways.

Aristotle was the first to define perfection, and he ascribed three related meanings: to be complete, to be so good that nothing of the kind could be better, and to attain one's purpose. These definitions illustrate the foolishness of trying to achieve perfection without Jesus. Only through his life, death, and resurrection can we be completed or attain our purpose. We can only be deemed good through his goodness.

When Scripture exhorts us to "be perfect," the phrase has little to do with performance or personal achievements—it is a call to allow ourselves to be completed in and by Christ. So the next time you are fretting about a personal imperfection, remember the words of St. Thérèse of Lisieux, who proclaimed, "I learned very quickly . . . that the more one advances, the more one sees the goal is still far off. And now I am simply resigned to see myself always imperfect, and in this I find my joy."[30] Like her, you can embrace your mistakes as a part of God's perfect plan for you!

Lord, thank you for your perfect love, which completes me! ⌐

Just for Today: I will deliberately tolerate a mistake (mine or someone else's) and reflect on the experience.

Letting the Love Out

Since God loved us so much, we also ought to love one another. No one has ever seen God; if we love one another, God lives in us, and his love is perfected in us.

—1 JOHN 4:11-12

Have you ever seen the magnificent sight of the sun's rays breaking through a storm cloud? They filter down in a fan of light that looks as if the very splendor of heaven is shining down on us. It looks like the fingers of God are reaching out in compassion to embrace humanity. One young child described this beautiful sight as the way "God lets the love out of heaven."

What a wonderful perspective! We could also say that each time the priest opens the tabernacle to bring Jesus to us in Communion, he is letting God's love out. This is when heaven meets earth, the mysterious way we see and experience God here on earth. When we let God's love seep into and saturate our hearts through our communion with him, we are infused with a supernatural grace that gives us the strength and wisdom to let the love out of our hearts to touch and minister to others.

God's love can break through our inner clouds, even when we don't feel very loving or are unsure of our ability to love. The late Pope John Paul II wrote, "Those who have come into genuine contact with Christ cannot keep him for themselves. . . . Christ must be presented to all people with confidence."[31]

In what ways are you being called to present Christ to others? What is holding you back? Do you lack confidence? Many people resist sharing Christ with others, out of fear that they are unqualified or unworthy. These are legitimate concerns, but presenting Christ to others doesn't require a degree in theology. People just need to hear how Christ has touched you. People need reassurance that God is loving and not too far away. You can bring them closer to God's love just by telling them your story of how Jesus has loved you.

Heavenly Father, show me the way to let your love out of my heart to touch others. Perfect your love in me. ⟶

Just for Today: I will be open to an opportunity to tell someone about God's love.

Getting off the Guilt-Go-Round

He will also strengthen you to the end, so that you may be blameless on the day of our Lord Jesus Christ.

—1 CORINTHIANS 1:8

Many women say that they feel trapped in a perpetual state of guilt. For those who work outside the home, guilt creeps in because they are not at home to raise their children. For women who stay home, guilt can feed a sense of inadequacy or insecurity if the family income is tight or others pressure them to use their talents to make a more "public" contribution to society. For women who are trying to do everything well, guilt comes from all directions when they fall short in any one of their roles.

While this may seem like a no-win situation, we *can* get off the guilt-go-round today! We can do this by believing that the Lord honors our best attempts at obedience and recognizes the sacrifices we make every day. The key to our sanity and spiritual well-being is seeking a balance for our lives that takes into consideration all of our obligations and respects our best attempts to prioritize them.

Women of faith have the same pressures, problems, faults, and fears that other women do. Even so, we think that with God on our side, we ought to handle everything with perfect peace and grace. The reality is that Christian women get fired, get depressed, go through divorce, get angry, and otherwise exhibit all the frailties inherent to being human. So why are we holding on to impossible standards and unrealistic expectations for ourselves? When is enough, enough?

Guilt is never a good motivator when it is excessive and fueled by external comparisons with others. In fact, it can do significant internal damage if it is left unchecked. Authentic, healthy, "good" guilt leads us to take swift action toward redemption, not condemnation. Likewise, guilt that is positive is experienced as a gentle nudge rather than as a repeated, bludgeoning blow to our conscience.

It's a grace to know the difference, and it's important to rid ourselves of guilt that keeps us in bondage. If you've let unresolved guilt define you or your life direction thus far, it's time to get off the guilt-go-round and start living in the land of God's infinite grace.

Lord, free me from the bondage of unnecessary guilt. ⸺

Just for Today: I will offer myself forgiveness and seek healing from unresolved guilt.

Roots of Rejection

"Anyone who comes to me I will never drive away."
—JOHN 6:37

An early experience of rejection can have a profound effect on the course of our lives. Whether it is real or imagined, experienced through abandonment or death, this rejection will color the way we look at the world, relate to others, and see ourselves. Rejection's roots can wrap around our hearts to undermine our emotional growth and spiritual freedom.

Even as we grow into adulthood and come to terms with the inevitability of rejection, our initial experience still has the capacity to deeply wound and bind us. Until we are able to face the original pain of the betrayal and gently bring it into our present, it will improperly constrain our ability to give and to receive love.

Through the help of spiritual guides, authentic friendships, and the presence of Christ in the Eucharist and in the Sacrament of Reconciliation, the Holy Spirit can unearth the roots of rejection that are sometimes so deep that we aren't even aware of them. When we commit to the path of freedom from these fears, we will no longer need to look outside ourselves for affirmation